Praise For Ray Edwards and *Writing Riches*

"Get 3 Copies"

"Grab your mouse and get 3 copies. Get one copy for yourself. One for your favorite vendor. And one for someone who still doubts that online copy is the "DNA" to accelerate business growth."
Alex Mandossian, CEO/Founder
AskAlexToday.com

"One Of The Best Living Copywriters Today"

"The words 'Ray Edwards' and 'World Class Copywriting' have the same meaning to me. He is simply one of the best living copywriters today."
Mike Filsaime
MikeFilsaime.com

"Superior Understanding of Human Psychology"

"In Writing Riches, Ray demonstrates a superior understanding of human psychology. He expertly shows you how you can use this understanding to share your message with your prospects and customers in a way that is meaningful for them. This is sure to help you to get your message out to more people and be more profitable online.

Ray uses time-honored tactics, which are updated for the new medium of the Internet. You hold a very powerful book in your hands—use it wisely."
Kenny Handelman, MD, Psychiatrist
TheADHDDoctor.com

"Lightning in a Bottle"

"Ray Edwards has caught lightning in a bottle! Writing Riches peeks behind the curtain into the future of copywriting, by guiding you, step-by-step, towards writing the most influential copy this side of Robert Collier. Masterful, elegant, and powerful—you will not be able to put it down!"
"DJ" Dave Bernstein
InterviewsForSuccess.com

"Get This Book!"

"Ray Edwards is a man of impeccable integrity and it shines through in his copy and now in his book. In <u>Writing Riches</u>, Ray takes you right to the heart of copywriting—what it is and, most especially, how to do it—with none of the verbal fog of most how-to books. Ray invites you into his inner sanctum where he opens his real-world copywriting tool kit. If you don't write your own copy Ray will show you how to get the very best work from those who write for you. If you do, Writing Riches is sure money in your bank. What else can we say except—Get This Book!"

Judith Sherven,PhD & Jim Sniechowski, PhD
Authors of Amazon #1 bestseller "The Heart of Marketing"

"An Instant Classic"

"Well, Ray, there goes my afternoon. I just read the first few chapters of your book and know I'm not going to get anything else done until I've finished the whole thing! I especially found the chapter on bullet writing brilliant—no one ever talks about it and it's so critical to the success of your online sales copy. Can I add your book to my classic marketing book website SFSBookstore.com? I think you've written an Instant Classic."

Bret Ridgway
SFSBookstore.com

"No Better Copywriter. Period."

"Ray Edwards has written marketing copy for me that was directly responsible for putting millions of dollars in my bank account. No better copywriter. Period. I can't believe he's putting his best secrets into a book, considering the fact that I pay him $30,000 to write a single promotion. Get this book. Now."

Matt Bacak
MattBacak.com

"Easy To Follow Your Steps"

"I wish you had come out with your book a couple of years ago before I spent $1,497 for someone else's copywriting course. Your book grabbed my attention and showed me more real life examples than that course did! You spell it out from real experience and make it easy to follow your steps to creating online copy that sells. Thanks for writing such a great book!"

Wade Thomas
DomainCoach.com

"Fireworks and Insights!"

"Finally, a copywriting book geared towards the modern world of web marketing! Ray's writing style so clear that it's easy to follow his models. I can't wait to apply these frameworks and insights to my online sales letters and watch my revenues double!"

Darrin Clement
WorldFitnessNetwork.com

"This Is A Must-Have Book"

"Using Ray's Sales Letter Building Blocks has taken away all of the anxiety and has helped me knock out sales letters in a fraction of the time they used to take before. AND… now they actually convert sales! It doesn't matter where you are with regard to writing copy, this information will take you to the next level… If you're just getting started, it will eliminate your fear and remove the roadblocks. If you've written lots of copy, this process will help you write faster and better and get you greater results. This is a must have book for any business owner that's serious about marketing their products or services."

Heather Seitz
EmailDelivered.com

"This Book Is Truly Awesome"

"Ray, WOW this book is truly awesome. You've explained a complicated and difficult process in very simple to understand terms. The way you then summarize with easy to follow checklists allows me to emulate your creative genius. Thank you so very much for sharing your experience and knowledge of copywriting."

Josef Mack

chbs-llc.com

"Don't Write Another Word Without It!"

"It's like having Ray Edwards sitting right next to you, showing you exactly how to write results-pulling sales copy. Jam-packed with step-by-step techniques and copywriting insights, Ray backs them up with example after example (even dissecting the copy of some of the world's top marketers to reveal why it works.) This book has earned a permanent spot next to my computer… Don't write another word without it!"

Lisa Suttora

LisaSuttora.com

"Worth Its Weight In Gold!"

"This book is worth its weight in gold! You will not find a more complete guide to writing web copy for your online business."

Frank Deardurff III

FrankDeardurff.com

"I Love Ray's Book"

"I love Ray's book on copywriting. He covers the basics in a clear way, and connects the primary role of the copywriter to the needs of the audience, and then goes on to an in depth explanation specific uses and applications of copywriting."

Douglas Samuel

DouglasSamuel.com

"Definitely Over-Delivers"

"Ray is a great teacher because he is a great student—what he teaches he has sweated out beforehand. He expects a lot from himself and you benefit big time from his expectations. He definitely over-delivers on whatever he does—like this book. This book is a must-have reference for anyone doing business on the Internet."

Harold C. Avila, DDS, MS
TMJagony.com

"Y-O-U Can Write Copy…Get This Book Today!"

"Y-O-U can write copy—that's the message that Ray Edwards conveys with <u>Writing Riches</u>. And boy does he deliver! If you want to improve the results from your email, your ads, or your salesletter, get this book today."

Jeanette S. Cates, PhD
JeanetteCates.com

Writing Riches

Learn How to Boost Profits, Drive Sales and Master
Your Financial Destiny With Results-Based Web Copy

RAY EDWARDS

NEW YORK

Writing Riches

Learn How to Boost Profits, Drive Sales and Master Your Financial Destiny With Results-Based Web Copy

ISBN 978-1-60037-755-6

Library of Congress Control Number: 2010921723

Morgan James Publishing
1225 Franklin Ave., STE 325
Garden City, NY 11530-1693
Toll Free 800-485-4943
www.MorganJamesPublishing.com

Dedication

"Anything in this book that is good, belongs to Jesus Christ. Anything in this book that is less than good you can credit to me."
  Ray Edwards

"Provide yourselves with moneybags that do not grow old, with a treasure in the heavens that does not fail, where no thief approaches and no moth destroys. For where your treasure is, there will your heart be also."
  Jesus, From the Gospel According to Luke, ESV

Table of Contents

A Note To The Reader
From Joel Comm

Words mean things.

It's not what you say, it's how you say it.

The pen is mightier than the sword.

There's nothing like using words to demonstrate just how powerful words can be.

The fact is that the written word is a powerful thing.

By understanding and learning the skill of writing great web copy, you are empowering yourself not only with the ability to make more sales and grow your business, but also with the potential to inspire people and change lives.

It's a high calling and one that is not taken lightly by the author.

You are privileged to hold in your hands Ray Edwards' finest work. He is generous with his teachings and holds nothing back. Be sure to take advantage of the opportunity to sharpen your sword and let your genius copywriter within you come forth to make an impact on the web and in the world.

Joel Comm
New York Times Best-Selling Author
JoelComm.com

Foreword
By Michel Fortin

Copywriting is both an art and a science.

Very few people understand and intimately know how to skillfully apply both ends of the copywriting spectrum—from capturing hearts to capturing wallets, from applying human psychology to making sales, and from telling compelling stories to boosting conversion rates.

An even fewer number of people know how to explain it and explain it adequately, particularly in insightful, cogent, and practical ways. Especially when it comes to the elusive, rapid-pace, and ever-changing world of Internet copy, that number seems to be a diminishing one.

Consequently, those who understand and know how to clearly communicate what invigorates, inspires, and influences the Internet reader in a way that translates into tangible results—results that drive profits and can, in many cases, save entire —are rare gems.

Ray Edwards is one such gem.

I am stubbornly fastidious when choosing copywriters to work with me. In my 25 years as a marketing professional and direct response copywriter, I've worked with many writers. And truth be told, I've resorted to a select few.

I've had the pleasure of working with Ray Edwards on many projects, and I recommend him at every opportunity. If you're lucky enough to work with him as I did (although, being in such high demand, I'm confident it may no longer be possible), the results will undoubtedly surprise you.

Foreword

Not surprisingly, on the other hand, is Ray Edwards' latest tour de force, *Writing Riches,* which is an eye-opening tome that all copywriters, both amateurs and veterans alike, should digest. It's a skillful explanation of the various elements that go into good, solid, results-driven web sales copy, and how they all work together and flow into each other for maximum selling power.

Once you immerse yourself into this book, you will notice, as I have, that your mind will be racing with new ideas and bumped by the occasional epiphany. Much of the work is already familiar to me and will be to the more experienced. But even so, I've learned several concepts that will undoubtedly make my work simpler, my copy more persuasive, and my business more successful.

So if you're looking for "eyeball glue" that keeps readers riveted to your words while making your sales soar, *Writing Riches* is certainly for you. Start absorbing the wisdom it contains without a moment's hesitation.

Your bank account will show it.

Your customers will love you for it.

Your business will depend on it.

To your success,

Michel Fortin
MichelFortin.com

Introduction

"Make money online!"

You can hardly open your in-box or enter any kind of search term without being bombarded with ideas about how to make a million dollars in a ridiculously short time from home. Working part-time. In your pajamas.

Here's the big problem with those ads: *They're all true!*

There are thousands of people making boatloads of money every day on the Internet. Many of those people make their money by teaching others how to make money themselves. There are hundreds of programs and packages teaching you how to develop a product, build a Web site, and attract traffic to it. Some are really, really good. Most aren't worth the hard drives they're printed on.

There's one key element that many of those teachers are missing, however…

> ➤ One element that will make your online venture a huge success or a crashing failure.
> ➤ One element that most people ignore, or take for granted, or think that they don't need to learn.
> ➤ One element that has consistently remained the most important sales factor in the marketing realm for over a century.

That element is: *copywriting*.

What Is Copywriting?

Copywriting is actually a fancy way of talking about the method you use to sell whatever it is you're selling. It's really advertising.

Here's a well-known story about the definition of advertising.

In 1904, an unknown copywriter named Joseph E. Kennedy was sitting in a saloon. He scribbled a note and sent it upstairs to Albert Lasker, one of the most powerful men in the advertising world at that time. The note said, "I can tell you what advertising is. I know that you don't know." He had no idea that Lasker had been searching for the answer to this question for seven years.

Lasker's curiosity was sparked, so he met with Kennedy, who told him the three-word definition of advertising: "salesmanship in print."

This meeting changed Kennedy's fortune—within four years, he was making well over six figures as Lasker's chief copywriter. The nature of advertising was also forever changed.

I believe the same definition applies to copywriting.

Copywriting is simply *salesmanship in print*.

The Most Valuable Skill

There is virtually no other skill that can make you as much money as copywriting. Nearly all Internet millionaire gurus know this secret: More than their product, more than their traffic-generation techniques, more than their e-mail campaigns, more than who their joint-venture partners are, it's their copywriting that has made them rich. This book will teach you how to use that secret for yourself.

I have. For the last twenty-five years, I've written successful copy for hundreds of clients, including banks, real estate brokers, hair-transplant surgeons, auto dealers, insurance agents, radio stations, hot tub dealers, pet stores, furniture stores, TV stations, and high-tech firms. All my knowledge of the fundamentals of copywriting can be found here in this book. Every piece of the puzzle I used to make a high six-figure income is right here. At the end of this book, you will know all my best copywriting secrets.

Each chapter will cover a different aspect of copywriting and how to use those skills for your online business. The wealth of knowledge that you are holding in your hand could easily cost you tens of thousands of dollars if you tried to obtain it on your own.

I'm sharing it with you because I believe you're ready to step out of your comfort zone and take control of your own financial future. You could say to yourself, "This is just another bunch of hype," set this book down, and walk away. If you choose to do that, you'll probably always have a nagging question in the back of your mind: "*What if I had read that book? How would my life be different today?*"

If you do decide to read it, be prepared to learn the most valuable skill in the realm of marketing on the Internet. Be prepared to build a successful business with a long line of hungry clients. Be prepared to make more money than you ever have before.

Even in your pajamas, if you like…

WARNING!

The information supplied in this book is extremely powerful in that it gives you the ability to literally manipulate people's thinking and actions. I'm not being funny—I'm very serious about this! The ability to write good copy is one of the most powerful psychological tools known to man. If you purchase this book, you must promise never to use this material for nefarious purposes. There are too many people on the Internet doing that already.

Chapter 1

The Magic Building Blocks of Sales Copy That Sells Your Products Like Crazy

"He who has a thing to sell and goes and whispers in a well, is not so apt to get the dollars as he who climbs a tree and hollers."

—Author Unknown

No one can argue that the Internet is the most revolutionary commerce tool that we've seen in our lifetime. Millions of people spending billions of dollars every day. Simultaneously and instantaneously making business transactions with clients in Boston, Barcelona, and Borneo. It's easier now more than ever to build a business and make a comfortable, even an extravagant, living.

Piece of cake, right? "If you build it, they will come." Here's where most online marketers fail:

➢ They get a great idea for a product or service.
➢ They plan their business carefully.
➢ They set up a Web site and wait for the orders to start rolling in.

Guess what happens? *Nothing!* Most Web sites are like an Old West ghost town. You can practically see tumbleweeds blowing down the streets.

What went wrong? Nine times out of ten, they've lost sight of the fact that the single most important ingredient to their Web site is the *words*. You can have the coolest spinning, flaming, flashing, morphing graphics on your site and still not sell a dime's worth of product. The reason? *Words sell.* The most boring, black-words-on-white-background sales page will outperform a flashy, colorful site every time *with the right words*.

The first place to employ those words is your sales letter. This is the primary selling point of your Web site. This is where most decisions to buy are made. The typical sales letter has fifteen basic elements.

It's a formula.

And if you follow the formula, you will get predictable results. You will sell stuff.

The 15 Sales Letter Building Blocks

1) The pre-head.

The pre-head is also sometimes referred to as the eyebrow. I guess that assumes that you think of a sales letter as a face. Because it's a sentence fragment usually found at the top left of the sales letter, it may look a bit like an eyebrow.

It might look something like this: "Attention, Pug Owners!" Now, if you're the owner of a dog that belongs to the pug group, that's going to grab your attention quickly.

How do I know? Because I am a proud pug owner, and I can tell you that anytime I see something that's directed to pug owners, it's got my attention. I want to know: What do you have for me? What might I be able to spend my money on for my dog?

That's how the pre-head works. It is a short sentence fragment designed to grab the reader's initial attention. It works very well regardless of what your product might be.

If you have a product that's designed to help people learn to play guitar, the pre-head could simply be: "Attention, wannabe guitar students!" Or, if you have a product that's targeted toward people learning to fly airplanes, it could be: "Attention, student pilots!" Or, if your product is for parents whose children suffer from ADHD, it could be: "Attention, parents of ADHD kids!" I think you see the principle involved here.

You're targeting the prime prospect for your message and you're qualifying him or her. You're saying, in essence, "Do you belong to this group? If you do, this message is for you. Pay attention!" That's what the pre-head is about.

2) The headline.

The headline is the ad for the rest of the ad. Its job is to make the reader want to keep on reading—specifically, to get him or her to read the next sentence. That's all your headline has to do.

Studies show that you have about two seconds to grab the attention of people who are coming to your copy for the first time. That's how long it's going to take them to decide whether or not they're going to keep on reading. In many cases, they're going to click the button and they'll be gone.

So you've got to do your job well in the headline and really grab their attention and get their focus. You will frequently see the headline in larger type and sometimes in a different color (red is used most often). This truly is the ad for the rest of the ad. The headline is something you need to spend a lot of time working on.

What exactly do I mean by "ad"? Well, the kinds of Web sites that we're writing are Web sites that sell. Often they're referred to as a "sales letter" Web site, and what that means is that it's written in letter format as if it were a letter on paper. Often it's on one long, scrolling Web page.

This is the primary tool of the online marketer, because it's been pretty much proven to be the most effective tool. I refer to that as an ad, and I also refer to an e-mail that's trying to make a sale as an ad, and I also refer to a Google AdWords ad as an ad. Whatever copy you're writing, for the purposes of our discussion in this book, is an ad.

Each of those items that I just mentioned—the e-mail, the sales letter, AdWords—has a headline, so the principles apply, even though the execution may be somewhat different. You can compare this formula to just about any sales letter you encounter online, and I think you're going to see that they all follow it pretty much to the letter.

3) The deck copy.

Some people call this the subhead, but I think that's inaccurate because we have another block in our stack of building blocks that we're going to call a subhead. So I want to distinguish that from the deck copy, which comes right underneath the headline.

The deck copy will be a block of type that is usually in black bold type and set apart from the rest of the text. It comes between the headline and the beginning of the letter.

The job of the deck copy is to reinforce the impact of the idea proposed in the headline and to also arouse more curiosity.

4) The body.

This is the bulk of your text. This comprises most of your sales letter. It also contains all the other elements that we're about to list. You can almost look at these top four as the main elements of the letter and the remaining parts as sub-elements that fall within the body.

Before we move on with the list, let me say a word or two about how to do the research necessary to write your ad. The first thing I would do is a simple Google search on your product and also on your target market (example: search "pug" as well as "pug owner," "pug lover," "pug training," etc.). Try to form in your mind what your market is looking for and start searching for keywords that they might use In other words, pretend you're a pug owner wanting to find out what's available for your pooch.

Another way to do it is to think about the generic terms used for the product category that you're working with and take those generic terms and combine them with the word *forum*. That's a great way to find places where people are discussing your topic online. You can just lurk, read the threads in the discussion forums, and see what people are talking about and what topics keep coming up over and over again.

If you find teleseminars hosted in the market that you're writing copy for, get on those calls and listen to the questions that are asked. If they're "real-world" seminars, go to those seminars and talk to people who are there—not about your product but about their problems. Especially attend the question-and-answer sessions at real-world seminars. Listen to the questions that people are asking.

There's a somewhat famous story about Armand Morin—who is a huge success in Internet marketing—attending one of his first seminars. He was taking notes but not very many notes. Someone with him asked, "Armand, aren't you getting much out of this?"

He said, "It's great! I'm getting a lot out of this!"

His friend said, "But you're not taking very many notes."

He said, "Oh, I'm just writing down the questions that people are asking. That's how I'm going to know what products to create."

5) **Subheads.**

These are smaller headlines that separate the major sections of your sales letter. I refer to them as the "bucket brigade" of your copy.

In the olden days before there were automobiles and big red fire trucks, there was the bucket brigade. This was simply a group of people who would run down to the river or the lake and form a line between the water and the burning building. They would stand within arm's reach of one another, passing the buckets back and forth, refilling with water and dousing the fire.

The person nearest the water would scoop up a bucket of water and hand it to the next person in line, and it would get passed along until it reached the burning building. Then the bucket would be returned to be re-filled. That's how they would put the fire out.

I'd like to take credit for inventing the bucket brigade theory of copy ... but I can't. I don't know if David Garfinkel is the person who originated that terminology or not, but he's who I heard it from first.

The subheads act like your own bucket brigade. They lead your reader through the body of your copy to get the gist of your message. My good friend and colleague Michel Fortin would tell you there are three things that prospects who read your copy never do at first (notice he said "at first"; it's the job of your copy to change that!).

They never read anything at first; they never believe anything at first; and they never do anything at first. The explanation of what that means is simple. At first they're not going to read your letter. At first they're going to glance at your headline and decide whether you're getting any more of their attention.

If you hold their attention, then there are three things they're going to do next. They're going to "skim, scroll and scan" (again, credit goes to Michel Fortin). They're going to skim through your letter and see if there's anything of interest to them. They're going to skim your subheads to get the gist of your story.

They're going to scroll down your letter as they skim, and they're going to scan it for things that they are interested in. If you can capture their attention while they're doing this, you've overcome the first thing they never do. Remember, they never *read* anything at first. If, and only if, you've captured their attention during this process of "skim, scroll and scan" with your powerful headline and persuasive subheads, they will go back to the top of your letter and begin to read.

The second thing people never do is they never *believe* anything at first. So now that they're reading, the job of your copy becomes to overcome their disbelief and skepticism and tell them the story they wanted to hear from the beginning.

I had a conversation with somebody today, talking about the difference between manipulation and persuasion. In my book, manipulation is using tricks to convince people to do things they didn't want to do in the first place, things that are not in their best interest.

Persuasion, on the other hand, is using tactics to persuade people to do something that is in their best interest and that they wanted to do to start with.

Think about your own experience when you're online and searching for something, perhaps a copywriting course. At first, you're going to "skim, scroll and scan" the Web site and decide if this is for you. When you see there are some things that interest you, you stop and begin reading.

What you really want is to be convinced that this copywriting course will answer your questions and provide you with the ability to make more sales.

That's what your prospects want as well. That's the difference between manipulating them and persuading them. If you can get past the fears that cause them to object to doing what you ask them to do, then you can move them to the next of those three things that people never do at first, which is people never *do* anything. They never buy anything at first, but if you've overcome the first two, overcoming the third is often just a matter of asking, so the subheads serve as the bucket brigade that moves that process along.

6) The lead.

This is the beginning of the body of the sales letter. This is the part that comes after "Dear Friend." It can be one paragraph, two, or several. Sometimes it consists of a simple "if, then" statement; sometimes it consists of a story that is intended to persuade you to think in a certain way.

The lead sets the criteria for whom the letter is intended and what they stand to gain by reading it. Think of the classic lead, which goes something like this: "If you've struggled to lose weight, if you've tried every diet imaginable, if you've taken every pill, if you've tried exercise routines, machines and personal coaches and you still haven't taken the weight off; then you're about to read the letter you've been waiting for all your life. Here's why:"

That's a lead. Does it do what we just talked about? Does it set the criteria for the intended reader? Does it tell you what you stand to gain by reading the letter? Apparently it's going to tell you how to lose the weight even if you've tried all this other stuff that never worked. It doesn't say, "The reason you won't lose the weight is because you won't stop eating!", but that's a different discussion.

7) Rapport.

What we mean by rapport is relationship building. People like three kinds of people: one, those who are like themselves; two, those who are like the way they would like to be; and three, those who like them back. Those are the keys to building rapport. Rapport is building your relationship, a friendly relationship that makes a person feel understood and valued.

Rapport demonstrates that you know the reader's pain, that you understand his or her problems, and that you have some common experiences that you can share that proves you understand his or her pain.

Dr. Stephen Covey's book *The Seven Habits of Highly Effective People* says that one of those habits is to seek first to understand then to be understood.

That's what building rapport is all about. This should not be a manipulative process. It can be used for those purposes; however, I hope that you won't.

All these techniques that we discuss, these psychological tactics, are powerful motivators of human behavior. I hope you understand that when I tell you that I want you to promise to only use them for good purposes, I mean it. These very tactics that we use in writing good sales copy, persuasive sales copy, can also be used to manipulate other people to do things that are not in their best interest.

I refuse to use these tactics that way, and it is my hope that you will as well. Rapport building is a powerful tactic for persuading certain behaviors, so use it with care. We're going to spend some time later going through some principles of rapport and some very specific tactics you can use to build it, including certain kinds of stories you can tell and certain kinds of mental constructs that you can set up in your prospects' minds that will put them more in your camp without them even realizing it.

8) Credibility.

You often see this section of a sales letter started with a subhead that says, "Who am I and why should you listen to me?" That's a classic subhead line that is often used by marketers. It works. You must build credibility with your prospects in order for them to lower the resistance they're naturally feeling.

People are afraid. When they're shopping online, they're afraid of giving you their credit card numbers. They're afraid of giving you their e-mail addresses, their contact information. They're afraid you're going to rip them off. One of the keys to overcoming this fear is to establish your credibility.

Establishing your credibility will answer the top question that they have once they've started reading your letter and that is, "Why should I listen to what this person has to say?"

9) Bullets.

A bullet is a brief statement that identifies a single benefit offered by your product or service. It usually doesn't reveal how that benefit is derived.

What do I mean? First of all, the reason they're called bullets is because they often appear in bullet point fashion on a sales letter. That's because bullet points are extremely scannable; they're easy to read. There's lots of white space around them; they're short; they're punchy; and if you format them correctly, someone can gather a lot of information by scanning over bullets very quickly.

Copy that converts at a high rate (makes a lot of sales) usually has a lot of bullets. Bullets are very powerful sales tools, and I'm going to urge you to use quite a bit of them. That's why we will spend an entire chapter on writing bullets and how it's done. There are some very specific techniques that I think you're going to find very helpful.

Want an example of a great bulleted list? Here's one from a sales letter written by Clayton Makepeace (he's the highest paid copywriter alive):

<Begin excerpt>

Close the deal fast! My stunningly simple secrets for closing more sales in a month than most writers do in a year.

a. You'll discover the six foundations of a powerful close.
b. Seven never-fail closing themes that work for any assignment.

    c.   Plus two closing blunders that could cost you everything at that final decisive moment.

<End excerpt>

Now, don't you wonder what those are?

That's the purpose of a bullet, to create that curiosity reaction that makes you think, "I've got to know what that is!" Think about your own experience with buying products from Web sites. Have you ever bought a product because you just had to know what one specific bullet was talking about? I have! I'll raise my hand.

10) Testimonials.

This is third-party verification that your solution does what it claims to do. These third parties are credible people who know. In other words, people who have used your product or service, liked it, and are willing to endorse it.

We've all seen them. We've all seen testimonials used. Most of us probably know by now that just using someone's initials in a testimonial is not as effective as using his or her full name.

You know if I have a testimonial on my Web site that says, "Ray is one of the best copywriters I've ever seen, and I've never hired anyone else to write copy for me until I hired Ray," and the initials below it say "J.W.," it's not nearly as effective as if the name below that quote is "Jeff Walker." It would be even more effective if we had Jeff Walker's Web site address and some audio or video from Jeff Walker.

Why is that? It's more believable. The most believable testimonial is one that is done on video and obviously not done by an actor. We can all tell when a real person gives a truly heartfelt testimonial on video as opposed to when an actor or actress gives a testimonial. So, you want to make your testimonials as believable as possible. Usually that means getting a video testimonial.

The next best thing is to get a photograph of the person, not a studio shot, but a candid shot, and include his or her full name and Web site address or, even better, his or her phone number. Most people won't agree to do that, and you must be respectful of that, but clients of mine who have used testimonials with phone numbers report that very few people actually call the phone number. Those who do just want to determine if it's a real person, so the calls are generally very short.

Using the phone number of someone who's giving you a testimonial really enhances the believability of that testimonial. This starts to tie a lot of the elements of a sales letter together. The testimonial enhances believability, which enhances credibility, which means people let their guards down, which means it's easier to build rapport and to get them to accept your lead in the premise of your headline. Do you see how these things begin to weave together? That's how we form the fabric of a good sales letter.

Now, if you're just starting out, of course, you may not have any testimonials yet. In this case, you could use quotes from famous people, as long as it's clear you're not implying that the famous person is personally endorsing your product. (If he or she is, good for you!)

For example, if you have a product about doing better advertising, you could include this quote from Mark Twain inside a testimonial box: "Many a small thing has been made large by the right kind of advertising."

Now, that isn't specifically about your product, but it supports your premise that advertising is important and it can make a difference in your business. Besides, it's from Mark Twain! People will read that and think, "Mark Twain's a genius. This guy must know what he's talking about!"

You can also use quotes from articles in research from credible sources. If you have a quote from a story you saw on

CNN, you can use that, as long as you stay inside the boundaries of fair use. You can't steal someone's copyrighted material, but you can certainly use quotations from people in authority that would be persuasive with your audience.

11) Value justification.

This is where you start to talk about how valuable your product, service, or solution actually is to the user. You highlight the value to your offer and do it in a way that contrasts it favorably to the price. Here's a good example:

If you are selling a course that teaches people how to save at least $10,000 on their income tax, then talk about the fact that they're going to save at least $10,000 and some people will even save $14,000, $20,000—or whatever those numbers might be.

Then when you talk about the price of your product being $500, that contrasts very favorably with the $10,000 in savings. I mean, really, who wouldn't hand over $500 in order to get $10,000 back? Jay Abraham teaches that principle this way: "Would you give me a quarter if I give you a dollar in return?" That's the value proposition that you're trying to set up, or "value justification."

12) Risk reversal.

We've gone through this whole process of getting the reader's attention, building the case that we have a solution to his or her problem, leading him or her to the place of building rapport, establishing our credibility, showing him or her all the benefits of our product, showing him or her how it's worked for other people, and establishing how valuable the product could be. Now we come to the real crux of the matter: removing any sense of risk-taking that our prospect may be feeling.

The simplest form of risk reversal is simply to say you have a 100 percent money back guarantee. You're telling them, in effect, "Try the product. If it doesn't work, you get your money back, so what have you got to lose?"

Now, of course, you have a couple of things to overcome. First of all, people have heard the phrase "100% money back guarantee" so often that it has become audio wallpaper to them. It has lost a lot of its meaning because it's been used so often—it's almost a cliché.

Your job is to find a way to express the guarantee or the risk reversal in such a way that you're taking all the risk off their shoulders and putting it onto yours, so that they feel they're taking no risk at all.

Frank Kern was the first person that I know of who really put this principle to work when he was selling e-books. Instead of just saying, "You get a 100% money back guarantee when ordering my e-book," he said something to this effect: "Download my e-book, read it, and if you don't like it, then just e-mail me and I'll give you all your money back. I'm taking a risk by doing this. I can't make you give the e-book back. I can't get the atoms back off your computer when you download the digital e-book, so you could just order the e-book, ask for a refund and rip me off, but I'm going to trust that you're not going to do that to me." In those few sentences, Frank made it obvious that the risk was really all his.

The risk was not being taken by the prospect at all. And yes, it's true, a certain percentage of people will do exactly what Frank said, they will rip him off by downloading the e-book and immediately asking for the refund, but not most people— most people are honest.

By describing the situation in those terms, it's really not any different than saying they have a 100 percent money back guarantee. It's just using language that more vividly illustrates the fact that the seller is taking all the risk, not the buyer. That's what risk reversal is all about—making it very clear that you're the one taking the risk, not the buyer. By doing so, you remove one of the biggest obstacles to making the sale.

13) The bonus.

Your bonus is a related but unexpected gift that enhances the value of your offer. I want you to think carefully about what I just said—it's unexpected. Those of us in the marketing world expect there's always going to be a bonus, so we don't count, but in markets that are not accustomed to seeing sales letters or not accustomed to studying them, they're often surprised.

In fact, they're usually surprised. Let's say you're selling an information product, a course on how to lose thirty pounds in thirty days, and people are reading your sales letter, which says you're going to give them instruction on how to do this very remarkable thing: lose thirty pounds in thirty days. They notice at the bottom of the page that you're offering a bonus. It's a workbook. This workbook will give them a place to record their progress, and it's absolutely free, if they order today.

It's worth $19, but you're going to give it to them for free. Now, that's an unexpected bonus; it's related to your primary offer, and it's valuable. It increases or enhances the value of your offer. That is a good bonus. The mistake I see people making in their online sales letters is offering bonuses that are not related to the product that they're selling and that don't enhance the value of their product.

Think of the bonus as the "extra degree." Here's what I mean: it takes 212 degrees of heat to boil water, so you could be at 211 degrees and the water is not boiling. That's the situation you're in with your prospect who's reading your sales letter. If you've done all the other parts right, you're at 211 degrees and you need to find a way to get that extra degree to make that water boil, to make the sale happen. Your bonus is that extra degree, that extra nudge that pushes the prospect over the edge.

14) The offer.

Or the call to action, as it's sometimes called. This is simply where you ask for the order and tell the reader what to do. You say, "Okay, these are the details of what I'm selling you, and here's what you need to do: click this button and order now" or "Order your copy now" or "Download this product immediately" or "Get instant access." However you're going to phrase it, you're basically saying, "Okay, now it's time for you to buy. I've explained all the reasons why; now you need to buy it."

Oddly enough, this is often a place where people take a step back and become shy and reclusive, not as aggressive as they should be in asking for the sale. By the way, this also happens in real-world sales—face-to-face selling. Often a salesperson will be at an appointment or in an encounter with a potential buyer and will go through the entire process of selling but won't ask for the sale.

You have to ask for the sale in order to get it. I guarantee you'll lose 100 percent of the sales that you don't ask for.

15) The PS.

Don't underestimate this one.

I know it's kind of a cliché that online sales letters have five, six, or ten PSes. Don't engage in that nonsense. The research that I've done shows that either one or three PSes seem to work best. You certainly don't need any more than that.

I usually just use one. Here's why the PS is important: Remember that readers skim, scroll, and scan. They start at the top and scroll all the way to the bottom. Why? Because they want to know, "What is this person selling and how much is it?" and that's usually near the bottom of the page.

So, often they'll scroll all the way to the bottom, and if you put a good, properly formatted PS at the bottom, you can restate your entire proposition in one sentence. This is the place where you sum up the top benefit that your product offers and you give them a link to be able to buy it.

If you have the ability to track where your clicks come from, you'll find that often your sale comes from a click on the PS, so it's important that you have at least one PS on your sales letter and that it sums up the top benefit of your product and offers a link for people to click on so they can buy.

Those are, very simply, the fifteen basic elements of a sales letter. Other experts may have more components, or less, or different subcategories, but if you consult several and pool the results, I think you will come up with a list very similar to this one.

SUMMARY:
The Fifteen Basic Elements of a Sales Letter

1. **Pre-head:** Targets the prime prospect for your message and grabs his or her attention.
2. **Headline:** The "ad for the rest of the ad"; its job is to get the reader to keep reading.
3. **Deck:** Reinforces the impact of the idea proposed in the headline and arouses curiosity.
4. **Body:** The bulk of your text; it consists of all the elements below.
5. **Subheads:** Smaller headlines that separate major sections of your sales letter; the "bucket brigade" of your copy.
6. **Lead:** Sets the criteria of who this letter is for and what they stand to gain by reading it.
7. **Rapport:** Demonstrates that you know the reader's pain and understand his or her problem, and identifies some common experiences you have with the reader.

8. **Credibility:** Answers one of the reader's top objections to your proposal, "Why should I listen to this person?"

9. **Bullets:** A brief statement that identifies a single benefit offered by your product or service (but doesn't reveal how that benefit is derived!).

10. **Testimonials:** Third-party verification that your solution does what it claims to do, from credible people who know.

11. **Value Justification:** Highlights the value of your offer to the reader and contrasts it favorably to the price.

12. **Risk Reversal:** Removes the biggest obstacle to getting an order (the prospect's fear that you will rip him or her off).

13. **Bonus:** A related but unexpected gift that enhances the value of your offer; the "extra degree."

14. **Offer (Call to Action):** Where you "ask for the order" and tell the reader what to do.

15. **PS:** The place to sum up the top benefit of your product for your readers.

Chapter 2

Headlines That Grab Readers by the Eyeballs and Suck Them into Your Message

"If you can come up with a good headline and lead, you are almost sure to have a good ad. But even the greatest copywriter can't save an ad with a poor headline."

—John Caples

In this chapter, I want to focus on just one element of the sales letter. That element is the headline. Headlines are absolutely critical to the success of your ad, probably the most important part, in fact.

Ironically, the best way to arrive at a good headline is to write a lot of bad headlines. When I'm writing a promotion for a client or writing sales copy for myself, I will sometimes generate hundreds of headlines. Overkill? Maybe, but I consistently end up with headlines that work.

Before we go much farther, I want to clarify that when I talk about headlines, I'm also referring to deck copy and subheads. These perform the same basic function as the headline, which is to grab attention and compel the reader to keep reading. In fact, frequently my deck copy and subheads come from the numerous headlines that I generated and didn't use.

Let's start now with five key qualities of compelling headlines. Remember, the job of the headline is to capture people's attention and compel them to read the rest of the ad.

Obviously you can't always get all five of these key qualities into a single headline. But your goal should be, when you're writing your copy, to try to get as many of these qualities into the headline as possible without making it seem awkward or difficult to read.

Ready to write some headlines yourself? Well, I'm going to make it even easier for you. I'm going to give you nine effective headline templates that you can steal from me. That's right; I'm just going to turn my back and you can swipe them. I won't even press charges.

9 Templates for Better Headlines

1) The how-to headline.

This is a direct headline. It's a direct selling technique. The key to making this particular headline work is that you need to tie it to a benefit your reader cares about (related to your offer, of course). That may sound third grade, but you'd be surprised how often I find that even experienced marketers and copywriters make the mistake of not tying it to their offer in a way that is relative to the reader.

It may be as simple as, "How to lose 30 pounds in 30 days without really even trying." That's a simple example of a how-to headline.

Examples:

"How to Lose that Last 10 Pounds Once and For All!"
"How to Land a Job in 7 Days… Guaranteed."

2) The testimonial headline.

This one is just like the establishing-credibility component of killer headlines from earlier; it's just a little bit more difficult to pull off. But if you have a powerful and incredible testimonial that can immediately capture your prospect's attention that also summarizes the big idea benefit of your offer, then this is a very effective headline—especially in today's online marketing world where people are more skeptical than they have ever been in the past.

If you're competing in a market that is very competitive, you need to find ways to differentiate yourself from your competitors. Action plans number one and number two are to out-credentialize them!

In other words, if ten people are offering the same product or service that you're offering, then you need to find a way to clearly define what makes you different. On one of my sites, I have Mark Victor Hansen telling people, "Ray Writes, You Profit!" That differentiates me as a copywriter.

Whether you're selling services, as would a chiropractor, a dentist, or a graphic designer, or you're selling an information product or an audio, it doesn't matter. If you have a testimonial that says what your product is all about and what your benefit is and it's from a credible source, then by all means use it.

Try putting that testimonial in a "Johnson box." The Johnson box was invented by a direct marketer at the turn of the previous century who put some copy near the copy of one of his print advertisements inside a box. It improved the response to that ad. This particular marketer's last name was Johnson; hence, it became known as the Johnson box.

If you put your testimonial inside one of those boxes, it can stand on its own as your headline as long as it relates directly to your offer and it's credible. Don't forget, though, you need to support it with the deck copy.

Getting your testimonials may be easier than you think. You could give copies of your product to people to evaluate and ask them for their honest feedback. Keep it honest! You don't want to pay somebody for a positive testimonial. Make sure you're in compliance with all laws and regulations concerning your product.

When you see books come out with two or three pages of testimonials from famous people in the front, you may wonder, "How can that be? The book was just published!" It's because they sent pre-publication copies to these people and asked them to write a paragraph or two about their impression of the book.

Another way to do it is to have a pre-product launch sale. Sell your product for a ridiculously low price to entice people to buy it and try it out. Another tactic that can sometimes be used effectively is testimonials about you.

Let's say you're a consultant, for instance, and you have people you've worked with in the past. Now you've written a book about how to systematize your business.

Your consulting clients can't comment on your book because they haven't read it or used it, but they can comment on you and your services. You could simply have testimonials under the heading "What people are saying about Donald."

Once you start selling copies of your product, then I would urge you to build into your Web site a continuous system for requesting testimonials and feedback from your users.

You can do that through autoresponders. You can have a message that automatically goes out right after people have received your product and asks them for a testimonial. Then you can have it occur again after a timed sequence once they've had a chance to use it.

Tip: **Put your powerful testimonial at the top of the page in a "Johnson box" if it can stand on its own as your headline. Support it with deck copy (which is also a headline!).**

3) **The give-me headline.**
This headline is all about the promise. When you truly have an irresistible offer, this is a very strong headline that will

really grab people's attention. An example of this kind of headline would be something on the order of, "Give me 48 hours and I'll show you how to pay 75% less taxes on your next IRS tax return."

It's a transactional sort of headline. You're asking for something in exchange for powerful information or results that your prospects really want. Again, it needs to be powerful; the trap you can fall into is thinking that your offer is so wonderful, when in truth it's not very different in the minds of your readers from all the other offers that are similar in nature.

You have to be careful about falling in love with your own offer. This is often where hiring a freelance or professional copywriter to write your copy for you is sometimes advisable because often we can't see the differences ourselves.

We don't know how to differentiate whether our offer is truly remarkable or whether we're just enamored with it because it's ours. This is something that you need to have some real discernment about. This is where getting a good fresh set of eyes, from outside your company, is very important.

Examples:

"Give Me 30 Days and I'll Give You a Washboard Stomach!"
"Give Me Just 48 Hours and You'll Understand Calculus Better Than Your Math Teacher."

4) **The reason-why headline.**

This is another direct headline that offers specific reasons to consider your offer. Using numbers is something that's often done when using the reason-why headline.

Alex Mandossian pioneered this concept with his Teleseminar Secrets sales letter site. He actually started his sales letter a couple years earlier with the seven reasons why you might not decide to take his course. I thought that was extremely innovative, and I eagerly waited to see what the results would be from this marketing campaign. The results were stellar! It was a very effective technique.

Examples:

"7 Reasons Why You Must Invest in Commodities Now… or You'll Hate Yourself Later."

"The 3 Factors That Prevent You from Losing Weight… and What You Can Do about Them."

5) **The probing question headline.**

This is where you ask a question that focuses on the prospect's point of view. Now, you really need to be careful here and pay attention to your question to make sure it's coming from the prospect's or reader's point of view and not from your own.

This question needs to be a question that either your reader or prospect would like to know the answer to or that evokes a strong emotion in him or her. The only way you're going to be able to achieve that is by writing this probing question from his or her specific point of view. We'll delve into some more examples of this later. This is a bit tricky to write, but it's very effective when you do it correctly.

Examples:

"Do You Recognize These 7 Warning Signs of a Heart Attack or Stroke?"

"Did You Ever Wonder Why Doctors Don't Get Sick?"

6) **The dominant emotion headline.**

This is simply a headline that echoes an emotion your prospect already feels. There was a famous headline written in the health and wellness industry that was targeted toward people who were in their middle years, crossing the lines of being forty plus and beginning to experience the aches and pains and problems that come with getting older.

The headline simply was, "Are you sick and tired of being sick and tired?" That's a perfect headline that calls on the dominant emotion. It's also a probing question headline for those of you who were paying attention. It's a probing question that evokes a dominant emotion.

This is the kind of headline that really does what we talked about in the last chapter. Remember we said one of the things we want to accomplish with a headline is to join the conversation that is already taking place inside the prospect's head?

That's definitely something that happens when you're using a dominant emotion headline like this one, because if you've got the right target audience reading this headline, then their response is, "Darn right I'm sick and tired of being sick and tired, and I wish somebody could tell me how to stop!" That's exactly the response you want your copy to get.

Examples:

"Are You Sick & Tired of Being Sick & Tired?"

"What the Internet Marketing Gurus Don't Want You to Know…That Keeps Them Rich, and You Broke!"

7) The command headline.

Again, you need to know your audience very well and be sure of what you're doing before you use this particular headline. When you're using it with the right readers, however, it can be very effective. You're simply telling your prospects to experience the benefit of your product. You're telling them what to do.

A really good example of this, which is one of my favorite mass market campaigns in the last decade or two, is the U.S. Army's campaign of "BE ALL THAT YOU CAN BE!" They changed it recently. Heaven knows why; it was ill-advised in my opinion. Now it says, "AN ARMY OF ONE," which makes no sense. Anyone who has been part of the armed forces knows that you're not encouraged to express your individuality.

But, "BE ALL THAT YOU CAN BE!" first of all evoked the real benefit that was in the minds of the prospects who were interested in joining the army. That is, they thought it was going to make them into the kind of person they couldn't have been otherwise.

They felt it was going to help them realize some great potential. They thought it could make them into a better person, someone who was more disciplined, someone who was stronger, who could achieve things and be part of something larger than themselves. So when you think of it in that context, you realize the headline "BE ALL THAT YOU CAN BE!" is a perfect expression of those emotions, that feeling, and the benefit they're seeking.

It's also a command. It doesn't say, "Do you want to be all you can be?" The headline doesn't say, "How to be all you can be." It simply commands you to do it.

Another famous headline that you will probably remember is one that was used by telecommunications giant AT&T. For a long time, they ran a campaign that contained a command, which was "Reach Out and Touch Someone."

Despite the fact that it became the source of a lot of humor from different comedians and late-night television shows, it was a command. It commanded people to experience the benefit of the product.

This is the most important message that I want to get across about this particular kind of headline technique. If you give commands that don't cause people to picture themselves experiencing the benefit of the product, it could backfire on you. Far from increasing your response, it will depress your response and lower the number of people who will act favorably on your proposition.

In AT&T's case, their campaign was a command that put people directly in emotional contact with the benefit, which was "You have the power to be in communication with those that you love, so what are you waiting for?"

They used to run ads showing a person who hadn't called his or her mother in a long time and then finally did. Once the person picked up the phone and called his or her mom, Mom was no longer depressed and living in a gray, dingy world, but rather a world of bright, vibrant colors. She laughed and smiled and there was love and the family was together, even though they were thousands of miles apart. All because of AT&T long distance. Awww, you've reached out and touched someone!

That's the kind of emotional connection you're trying to make with people, and this is how the command headline can do that. Think about this; this is not a business opportunity kind of copy. This is not a "how to make money" kind of copy or "how to make better investments" or "how to succeed and be an achiever." It's not about all that; it's all about emotions and connecting with people. Yet a command headline works in that space.

So, for instance, just because you're writing copy that might be intended to be read by women, and might be intended to make the more emotional sale, does not mean you can't employ these same techniques. I don't think you can find a greater difference than between marketing to people who want to join the army and marketing to people who need to call their mom. These are very different ideas you're trying to get across, yet both use the command headline tactic—which is why I included those two specific examples.

"Don't Make the Mistake Made by 90% of All Seniors—It Could Cost You Your Life!" This third example is an interesting one, as it begs the question, "What mistake?" It must be a specific mistake because it says "the mistake," and it's made by a lot of people. What could it be? Is it something to do with diet? Is it something to do with where I live? Do I need one of those emergency alert things or some kind of ID tag? Always join the conversation already going on in your reader's mind.

Examples:

"Be All That You Can Be"

"Reach Out and Touch Someone"

"Don't Make the Mistake Made by 90% of All Seniors – It Could Cost You Your Life!"

8) The if-then headline.

This is used a lot and yet it's still very effective. You simply contrast something that's easy for your prospect to do with the major benefit of your product. What does this mean?

Let's say you're selling a service that allows people to send video e-mail to one another, and to continue playing on the emotions that we were discussing in the previous example, maybe this becomes a way that people can send video postcards to their relatives. The grandkids can send a video to Grandma and Grandpa.

The concern there might be that Grandma and Grandpa might not know how to do the whole computer video thing. It might be too complicated for them, so a perfect if-then headline for that situation would be something like this:

"If you can send and receive e-mail, then you can get video postcards from your grandkids like clockwork every week."

You contrast something that's easy for Grandma and Grandpa to do. "Heck, we know how to send and receive e-mails! We've been doing that for at least a year. We finally got us one of them there computers!"

Well this says that if you can send and receive e-mail, then you can send and receive videos from your grandkids. You're simply contrasting how easy it is to send and receive e-mail with the idea of receiving video. Suddenly it doesn't seem nearly so daunting. That's a powerful headline for that type of market space.

Examples:

"If You Can Send & Receive E-mail, You Can Trade Online."
"If You Can Follow Simple Directions to Make a Recipe, You Too Can Make Web Pages for a Living."

9) **The warning headline.**

If you're writing a piece of copy, especially one that involves a serious problem, the warning headline can be very effective. It can grab people's attention, arrest them for a moment, and make them stop and read what you're saying, especially if you can combine some credibility evidence with your warning.

I was just reviewing a piece of copy that was written by Clayton Makepeace. It was about a nutritional supplement that helped relieve arterial inflammation, which is one of the major causes of sudden death from a heart attack. You may or may not know this, but recent studies revealed that over 400,000 people who had healthy arteries died each year from heart attacks.

Now, what have we been taught over the last two or three decades? We've been taught that if you don't eat right, then your arteries harden and they build up all this plaque and then you have a heart attack, which can be deadly. Now we're discovering that people who don't have hardening of the arteries, but rather have healthy arteries, can also die of a sudden heart attack. Why is that?

That's what Clayton used to lead into this brilliant marketing piece that he wrote, and it was the perfect opportunity to use a warning headline. You could write a headline that might say something like, "WARNING: Even Though Your Arteries May Be Perfectly Healthy, New Studies in the American Journal of Medicine Reveal You Might Still Die of a Sudden Heart Attack."

If you're of a certain age, that definitely gets your attention. "You mean I could do everything right; I could cut out all the foods I like to eat and take all these vitamins and supplements; and I could exercise, have healthy arteries, and still suddenly drop dead from a heart attack? What are you talking about? I need to know more about this!" Then you're off to read the copy.

That's how the power of a warning headline can work. It helps if you can bring in credibility, facts, and an article from the news. I don't mean the entire article in your headline; I mean a piece of information that is commonly known to have been in the news recently so people will recognize it when they see it and immediately connect your copy to the information they already have.

Examples:

"WARNING: What Your Doctor Isn't Telling Can Kill You"

"WARNING: Are You at Risk of Losing Your Life Savings Because of This Common Annuity Loophole?"

Wow, with all these different types of headlines, how do you choose? Well, I can't answer that for you, but I can tell you what works for me.

The short answer is, it revolves around finding what the hook or the big idea is for your copywriting project. I used to start my copy work by writing all the headlines first. I don't do that anymore; now the headline is the last thing I write. The reason is, while I'm in the process of writing the rest of the copy, I come up with all kinds of ideas. What I'm looking for is the one that jumps out at me and makes me feel like it is the big idea for the entire promotion.

The first thing I do is an in-depth phone interview with the client. I'll ask a lot of questions, record the call, and have it transcribed. Some of the questions to ask would be: "What's the story behind how you came to offer this product? Tell me the story of how you got here. What led you here? What did you do before? How did you come to be doing this? How did you come to have this idea or get this product or develop this information or start performing the service you're offering?"

If this is your own product, ask these questions of yourself. You'll be surprised sometimes at the unknown gems you'll uncover in your own history that can be worked into your copy.

For example, in my case, I'm a former radio disc jockey. I tend to downplay that part of my past; it doesn't seem relevant. But I find that any time I bring it up, people say, "Wow! What kind of disc jockey? Did you meet anybody famous? You met Shania Twain and Garth Brooks? What was that like?" The things that you might be bored with about yourself may fascinate other people and can become an interesting hook for your copy

Next, I do a lot of research. This involves looking at competitor's Web sites and competitor's projects, if they've done print advertising, and so forth. Then, I examine the product itself and make lots and lots of notes. All that will come together into a document that's really just a whole list of bullet points of thoughts that I have about this project. Then I start looking at those pieces and writing sections of the copy.

It's an organic process. Sometimes I start by writing the lead, if there's an obvious story. If the product was developed because of a personal story that happened with the owner/inventor, then I'll probably start by writing that story. If it's more about case studies of what people have gained by using the product or service, then I'll start by writing out that case study.

You can also make lists to help the process. One list could be six ways your product or service would surprise people who bought it. Your brain goes, "What? I don't know ... they'd probably be surprised that it actually works!" That's a valid answer—write that down! Don't judge your answers; just write down the answers that come to you.

List six features and six benefits of your product. Remember, the features are what the product has. If it's a car, it has titanium alloy wheels, a 12-valve engine, a tachometer, and a sunroof. The benefits are what the product does for you. If the car has a sunroof, the sunroof is the feature—but what's the benefit? The benefit is you can feel the wind coursing through your hair while you're driving down the road.

List six ways your product is different from competitors' products.

List six questions people may have before they want to buy your product.

List the six most common objections people might have to buying your product.

(By the way, there is no magic to the number six. It could be five or twelve or whatever.)

As you make out these lists, understand that each of those answers in front of you is a potential headline, subheadline, sentence, or paragraph in your copy.

Sometimes when I'm stuck and don't really know where to begin, I'll start by writing the actual offer and branch out from there and begin writing the other parts of the copy. Almost every time the headline is the last thing I write after I've written all those other things.

I go into the headline brainstorming process, and by that time I have lots of fodder that I can use to write all these nine different types of headlines. (There are actually dozens of ways to write headlines, but nine is definitely enough for most marketers' purposes to use for writing their own copy.)

When I get to the headline-writing stage of a project, I write lots of headlines, always over a hundred. I tend to write several versions in each of these nine kinds of headlines and then subjectively using my sixth copywriting sense (if there is such a thing), pick the ones I believe have the greatest likelihood of succeeding. Then, I look for the one that jumps out at me and feels like the big idea, and I subjectively decide in my mind, "That is the headline we're going to start with."

One last thing I want to address in this chapter is some common headline-writing mistakes. The number-one mistake is being focused on you and your product instead of on your prospects.

Your prospects don't care to hear about you. They want to know what all customers want to know: "What's in it for me?" Any time you see a headline that says, "We've got 20 years of experience!" or "We're the best in the business!" or "The number-one method for doing (x)" or any of those kinds of things, those are product-focused headlines or company-focused headlines. At best, these types of statements are claims. If your claim is, "We're the number-one split testing accelerator software," that's a great claim, but how do you back that up? Even more to the point, how does it benefit me as your potential prospect?

We could instead say, "How to double, triple, or even quadruple your Web page profits with the click of a button." Not a great headline, but it focuses on your prospects and their needs. Being focused on yourself rather than on your prospects is a huge mistake.

Another mistake is using clichés in your headlines. Now, I'm going to raise my hand and say I've been as guilty of this as the next person. Here's what happens. We get involved in writing copy to sell our products and services and we're taught to mimic the classic successful direct-response headlines.

Then suddenly there are thousands of sites all over the Internet that start with the words "Who else wants to…" That headline still works. It's still powerful, but its effectiveness has greatly diminished. So, it's approaching the point that in some market spaces, particularly the Internet marketing market, the "who else" headline is almost a cliché, a parody of itself.

Also, avoid using "adspeak" words. They are like red flags waving in front of the prospects' faces that tell them, "You are now reading an ad"—phrases like "45% discount" or "Today only special." More and more, the work that I'm doing for clients and the work I'm doing on my own sites is more of an "advertorial" approach.

By "advertorial," I mean it feels more like I'm supplying articles and interesting, helpful, and useful information than writing an ad. I think in today's over-communicated, over-advertised, oversold environment, it's more important than ever that you fly under that radar, and for heaven's sake, don't have little flashing lights on your airplane that say, "Here comes an ad."

SUMMARY:
5 Key Qualities of Compelling Headlines

1. **Grabs Attention.** Your headline's number-one job is to arrest the prospect's attention with a single "big idea."
2. **Screens and Qualifies Prospects.** Choose specific words that segment out the exact prospects you want to reach. Headlines that apply to everyone can just as easily apply to no one.
3. **Draws Readers into the Body Copy.** Your headline's job is to convince readers to ... keep reading.
4. **Communicates the "Big Idea."** What is the one true benefit of your offer, and how can you communicate that to your prospects? Put that into your headline.
5. **Establishes Credibility.** If you can establish some authority in your headline or pre-head, you will be far ahead of most copywriters.

Chapter 3

Magic E-mails That Make More Money

"Make it simple. Make it memorable. Make it inviting to look at. Make it fun to read."

—Leo Burnett

This chapter is all about autoresponders and e-mail marketing. The subject of e-mail marketing itself generates a little bit of controversy. Some people say e-mail marketing is dead, that it doesn't work anymore. Their supposition is that all the spam filters and so forth have made it impossible to market via e-mail. This is absolutely not true.

E-mail marketing still works. It's less expensive than using direct mail, but there is a cost involved. Some people labor under the illusion that e-mail marketing is free, but it's not. There is a cost to get your e-mails delivered at a good rate. There is also a cost in terms of time and effort if you want to create an effective e-mail marketing campaign. The good news is e-mail marketing definitely continues to work even in the age of spam filters.

The first thing you should do to build your e-mail marketing campaign is to start an e-mail swipe file. Remember in the last chapter I gave you permission to steal from me? In this chapter, it gets even better: I'm encouraging you to steal from other people, too!

A "swipe file" is a collection of copy that you know works. Copy that is effective and is making sales. Copy that you can study and learn why it works; then you can model it in your own promotions and copywriting in the future.

Of course you don't want to steal or plagiarize, but you can certainly model and use the form, structure, and ideas contained in your swipe file. The best way to start an e-mail swipe file is to pick successful e-mail marketers and get on their lists. That's a pretty simple way to learn from the pros.

The second thing you should do is write an autoresponder sequence. This is not as difficult as it sounds. One simple way to do it is to simply chop up your sales letter and send that out via autoresponder. I'd love to take credit for that idea, but I must tell the truth and credit my good friend and mentor, Armand Morin. We'll go over how to do this later on, too.

Your third step is to write out subject lines for your e-mails. Now you should be ready to do this because e-mail subject lines are in fact headlines, and you just spent a whole chapter on writing good headlines! True, subject lines are a little bit of a different art form, but if you are skilled at writing headlines, they should come easy to you. Later in this chapter, we'll take a look at some subject lines that work and why they work.

Whether you're writing on-page copy (sales letters, squeeze pages, etc.) or off-page copy (autoresponders, e-mail marketing promotions, and so forth), persuasion principles do not change.

People are still people. Regardless of whether they are online or off-line, they still respond to the same psychological phenomena, the same stimuli, and are influenced by the same factors. If you keep that in mind, you'll find that writing e-mail promotions and autoresponder copy is not that much more difficult than writing other kinds of sales copy.

OK, let's get started talking about the twenty-one keys to persuasive autoresponders and e-mails.

21 Keys for Better Email Marketing

1) Use e-mail marketing to build permission-based lists.

We're going to start at ground level discussing autoresponders and e-mail marketing, and we're going to build our way up from that foundation. The foundation of all e-mail marketing is "permission-based marketing." This is a term that was coined by Seth Godin, who is the author of many best-selling books, including *Small is the New Big*, which I recommend highly to you.

Really, any of his books should be on your bookshelf, but certainly this one. It has some great insights into online marketing and marketing communication in today's world. His most famous book is called *Permission Marketing*.

Permission marketing is Seth's term that simply means, "I have opted to receive your marketing messages. I give you my permission to market to me." We call that act an "opt-in." It sounds like a simple concept, but as we all know on the Internet today, we're often the target of marketing messages that we did not give permission to be sent to us.

The difference in how we respond to marketing that we did or did not give permission to receive is like night and day. When I receive a marketing communication that I did not give permission to be sent to me, my response is hostile at worst and ambivalent at best. Most often, I just hit the delete button and move on.

That's certainly not what we hope to have happen to our marketing materials. The way to get out of that particular scenario is to get permission from your prospects to market to them. How do we do that? The simplest method would be to place a subscription form on your Web site for people to sign up for your e-mail–based newsletter or to receive an occasional notification from you about promotions, products, or offers that you may have for them.

This was the way it was originally done about five years ago, and it was pretty easy. You put a form on your Web site that just said, "Sign up for my e-zine"; people signed up like crazy; and they were happy to do it. It doesn't work quite that simply these days because people are so buried in e-mail you've got to present more of an enticement to get them to opt-in to your list.

Remember this: people who have given you permission to market to them are the most likely people to buy from you. Think about how powerful that information is. It may seem like a no-brainer that if someone is willing to give me his or her name and e-mail address, asking for information, then of course he or she will be more likely to buy.

The truth is, these prospects, readers, and subscribers have done you an enormous honor by saying, "I trust you enough to give you permission to come into my e-mail box." Honor that permission. If you do, you will be able to widen the circle of permission.

They may start by giving you only their e-mail address. Eventually, they may buy your entry-level product and give you their mailing address or perhaps even their phone number. Then perhaps they'll buy bigger ticket items from you.

With each step, the circle of permission widens until you get to the point where they may in fact allow you to sell them something that you keep billing them for, month after month. That's called a continuity product.

Many of you may be interested in building a membership Web site. It's a great way to build continuing revenue. It's also a lot of work. You have to put a lot of effort into delivering value, or people won't stay subscribed to your membership site, but that's the ultimate form of permission. The ultimate form of permission is, "Keep billing me; I want to keep buying from you."

2) **Use a reputable e-mail delivery service.**
Many people getting started in this business of e-mail marketing look at all the different options and ask me, "Ray, should I buy a piece of software that I install on my computer and send those e-mails from my desktop, or should I get one of these programs

that I install on my Web server and it sends the e-mail out for me, or should I go to one of these third-party services like 1ShoppingCart, AWeber, GetResponse, or a different third-party autoresponder company?"

My answer is you should use a third-party service to deliver your e-mail marketing messages. The bottom line is if your e-mail doesn't get delivered to the intended recipients, you just won't make any money. So no matter how good your copy is, it will never be read. If it's never read, you don't make any sales.

The fact of the matter is, getting your e-mail delivered and keeping yourself off the spam lists (where your e-mails are automatically junked) and staying on the white lists (where your e-mails get through every time) is a full-time job.

Most people probably don't have the time and resources, nor the technical knowledge to make sure their e-mails are getting delivered every time. Services like AWeber.com or 1ShoppingCart.com have a full-time staff that works to get your e-mails delivered. They have rules about what they will and will not allow you to do.

For instance, they have rules about whether you can take a big file of e-mail addresses and upload it to their service and say, "Put this list of 5,000 people into my account." They won't let you do that without confirming that those people actually wanted to be subscribed to your e-zine. Is this a good thing? Yes, it's a very good thing! Keep in mind the concept of "permission marketing" and you won't be accused of spamming.

The bottom line is: working with a third-party service like AWeber or 1ShoppingCart will get your e-mails delivered and you don't have to worry about it. You're paying a very modest fee for professionals to take care of that for you.

3) Give Web visitors reasons to opt-in.

In other words, give them reasons to join your list. This might sound obvious, but I know that's one of the big questions that people have: "How do I build a list?" One way to build a list is by having a Web site that offers some sort of premium to entice visitors to give up their names and e-mail addresses. You have to offer people something they really want. For many of us, that means we're going to be giving them some kind of information or software, something in downloadable form.

Perhaps you've written a special report, or you have a PDF, or maybe you have a transcript you want to share with people. Some folks will have a piece of software that they'll offer to people who sign up to be on their mailing list.

It used to be that you could offer a special report or something of that nature, but now you have to work a little harder because people are more skeptical. They've seen these techniques before, so you have to work a little harder to get them to give you that contact information.

Simply make sure your special report has some really concrete information in it that's different from what everyone else is offering. In the last few years, a lot of people obtained the resale rights to a lot of the same e-books, and they gave those away.

Now, as people are surfing around the Internet, they see a lot of the same e-books over and over, so it's going to take more to capture their attention. Most of those e-books were about how to make money, so in that market, especially, you will have to work harder.

You have to come up with unique information. The best thing you could do is have proprietary information for products that you can give people to entice them to give up their names and e-mail addresses. So, just "sign up for my e-zine" is not going to cut it anymore; you've got to have something more valuable.

One option would simply be an audio recording. Have someone interview you on your area of expertise, or you can interview an expert. Just make sure it's someone who isn't an interview hound who's been interviewed by everybody and their brother. Remember: unique and proprietary.

It's best if you can find someone that people would like to hear from. Someone that's famous enough in your market that people would like to hear him or her, but not so famous that he or she is oversaturated and people are tired of hearing him or her. You could record that interview and then offer the recording as a premium for people who opted-in to your list.

4) **Avoid spam complaints with frequent consistent mailings.**
Getting your e-mails delivered is vitally important. If you want to avoid getting a lot of spam complaints from people, you need to mail frequently and consistently.

There's no quicker way to get a rash of spam complaints than to get people on a list, send them nothing for six weeks, and then send them an e-mail out of the clear blue sky. They may not even remember you! They will complain; they will hit that spam button; and you'll have another spam complaint.

The question then is, "How often should I mail?" Some of the most successful e-mail marketers—believe it or not—send an e-mail every single day. In fact, Matt Fury, one of the top e-mail marketers online, sends two e-mails a day. So does John Alanis, whom we discussed before.

Different people have different opinions about the ideal frequency for e-mailing. Some people say every two weeks, some people say once a week, some people say twice a week, but I've found a reasonable starting place for most people is probably twice a month. If you get down to mailing once a month, that's probably not frequently enough, although some people have had success with that.

Every other week seems to be a good interval, but the key is—regardless of how often you mail—do it consistently. Get in the habit of sending them out at the same time and on the same day. The more people become accustomed to expecting your mail on its designated day(s), at the same time of day, the more comfortable they will be seeing your name in their in-box, which means fewer spam complaints for you.

Finally, you can avoid spam complaints by not using spam words in your e-mails. Words that refer to the enlargement of certain body parts or to things like sex or specific pharmaceutical drugs, or even the word *free*, which has become a big no-no. A lot of spam filters are set to catch that word.

These kinds of words you need to watch carefully. If you're using 1ShoppingCart or AWeber, each of those tools provides a method, as part of your membership, to scan your e-mail for possible spam flags, so you can remove them and change the language to improve the deliverability of your e-mail.

5) **Use autoresponders as robotic sales agents.**

Too many people underestimate the power of autoresponders. One proven principle in marketing is that it takes a series of contacts to move people to a buying decision.

When they're first exposed to your product or offer, they are not as likely to buy as they are after three or four contacts. Many marketing experts say it takes as many as seven contacts before you're able to determine whether or not you've gotten the maximum number of sales in a marketing campaign.

So how are you going to make those seven contacts? The people who come to your Web site, look it over, and leave are people you have no control over. You have to leave it to chance that they're going to come back six more times to be exposed to your message. How many of us think that's likely to happen? I can't see you right now, but I imagine that you are not raising your hand. I hope that's not because you've put this book down, walked away, and will never come back!

Now, if they come to your Web site and they have a reason to give you their names and e-mail addresses, you can arrange for them to come back, because you can send them an e-mail tomorrow that says, "Ray, I sure do appreciate you stopping by my horse tack Web site. I've got a special on saddles today I thought you might want to take a look at. Here's a link:"

Then the day after tomorrow, you can send them another e-mail that says, "Ray, I don't know if you've noticed or not, but that sale on the saddles that I was telling you about yesterday is over tonight at 5:00 p.m., so if you really wanted one, you should come back and take a look. Here, click this link."

Obviously I'm oversimplifying the copy, but I think you see my point. You can set up your autoresponders so they do this for you automatically. You don't have to lift a finger for it to happen. The marketing sequence is set up in advance.

6) **Create a sequence that sells, using your sales letter copy.**
A sequence of contacts is the most powerful way of delivering your sales message. Once you get your sales letter copy written, you really don't need to write all of your autoresponders from scratch.

Simply chop up sections of your sales letter, do a tiny bit of editing, and send those e-mails out in sequence. How many should you send out? Armand Morin, whom I mentioned earlier, says somewhere between seven and eleven e-mails as a minimum number.

7) **Ask for the sale in every e-mail.**
This is one where I think people frequently miss the boat. There are times when strategically it's probably not a good idea to ask for the sale, but most of the time you need to give a link back to your most wanted result—your MWR.

If you're Armand Morin and you're promoting Big Seminar (his big marketing event of the year), you want people to click the link and buy a ticket to Big Seminar. You need to think about what that MWR is and treat each e-mail as if it were a miniature sales letter. One of the things I'm going to teach you about sales letters is you need multiple links to your buying process. You need the same thing in every single one of your e-mails. Don't forget to ask for the sale.

8) Craft a powerful signature file for all of your e-mails.

Your signature file is an action device. It is the little piece of text that your e-mail system automatically appends onto the end of your e-mail.

It is something that's often an afterthought. People don't think about the content they put in the signature file, but it's a perfect place to sell your offers with a link back to your sales page or to your other products, so give some careful thought to what copy you're going to put in your signature file. I propose you use it as one more opportunity to make a sale.

Many times people will scroll through your e-mail to the end, and if they see a link, they'll automatically click on it, so it's a good place to direct people where you want them to go. Don't overlook it.

You can also set up signature files in your desktop software as well, not just in your AWeber, 1ShoppingCart account, or Marketer's Choice, or whatever e-mail system you use.

You can have multiple signature files as well. In my Macbook's e-mail program, I have the ability to choose multiple signatures. It will actually rotate the signatures, so you can always make some kind of offer whenever you send out an e-mail. It doesn't matter whether it's a broadcast e-mail to your entire list or just an e-mail to a friend or business associate.

9) **Use broadcast e-mails for promotions.**

Broadcast e-mails are different from autoresponder sequences. I want to take a little bit of time explaining this, to make sure I clearly spell this out.

The autoresponder sequence is simply a robotic sequence of messages that's sent out by the computer once you sign up to be part of that particular mailing list. No human has to know that you signed up. Nobody has to click "send." It's all done automatically.

A broadcast e-mail is an e-mail that you, as the owner of the account, trigger to be sent to the list. Broadcast e-mails are not only good for information, they're also great to use for promotions, if you're doing a sale that's tied to a specific date.

For instance, if you're doing a Valentine's Day sale, or it's time for the big basketball tournament in your community this month, you could be doing a promotion in relation to that.

You can also use it to do launch sequences or time-bound offers. What I mean is, if you were going to have a "School's Out" promotion for your particular business and you know school will be out in May in many parts of the country, you could send a sequence of e-mails designed to drive sales of a particular product or service around that time-based event.

Once you have a certain date on the calendar that you have marked off, you do a sequence leading up to that. If it's a sequence of broadcasts, you can write in each e-mail things that come from today's news or talk about the weather, observations that can only be bound to time. People will feel a connection to you when you write about current events in your e-mails.

They may not think about it consciously, but something about that e-mail feels more personal, more real to them than some kind of automated e-mail sequence. It feels like you are relating directly to them—like you have shared experiences when you refer to things that are happening in the news, weather, and so forth.

10) Know your most wanted response.

This is probably the biggest mistake that I see being made in e-mail marketing. People send an e-mail and they don't know what they want the reader to do. Is it to click this link and buy the product? Is it to click this link and go listen to an audio file or watch a video, or is it to pick up the telephone and call a certain phone number?

What I typically see is an e-mail sent out to a list that has multiple calls to action or no call to action. These are both egregious marketing mistakes. You need to know what your MWR is for this particular e-mail and focus on it (which leads us to key number eleven…).

11) Use only one MWR.

A confused mind never buys. A confused mind doesn't want to make a decision. If you don't know what your most wanted response is, how on earth can you persuade someone else to take action?

12) Craft subject lines using the PAC formula.

PAC stands for personal anticipation and curiosity. You want to write your subject lines as headlines, and what's the job of the headline? It's to get people to read the rest of the ad.

What's the job of the subject line in an e-mail? In personal e-mails, often it would appear that the subject line's only job is to confuse us or to obscure the nature of the e-mail. If we're trying to sell things to people, we want to take the opposite tack and make it crystal clear.

We want to arouse curiosity and get people to read what's inside the e-mail. First of all, make the subject line personal. That could include putting someone's name in the subject line. Most of the e-mail providers like AWeber. com or NewMarketingAutomation.com—which is also 1ShoppingCart.com—offer a way for you to personalize that subject line, but that's not what I'm talking about.

Although I think you should do that, it's not as effective as it used to be because people are wise to that trick now. It used to be that you'd see your name in the subject line and think some human being actually typed in your name, which obviously must mean it was written specifically to you! Then you'd open up the e-mail and wonder, "How did this guy know I needed hair growth treatment?"

It's because you were the victim of an automated spam e-mail. So now people are a little bit wary—depending on how the name is used in the subject line. I don't recommend you stop using this tactic; I just recommend you be careful. The bottom line is you want to make your ad not look like an ad.

If you take nothing else away from this chapter but the determination to make your e-mails never look like ads, that would be a good thing.

Making that happen will get you the highest response rate of your entire marketing career, trust me. It's not as easy to do as it sounds. People's ad radar is very sensitive, but if there's any way to do it, it begins with this PAC formula.

Personal means not just sticking the name in the subject line—it means saying something that's meaningful to the person, that's directed precisely at what he or she is thinking about, what his or her desires, fears, and discomforts are.

In our PAC formula, the next thing you want is to fulfill anticipation. If, at the time you got the person to opt-in to your list, you created the right anticipation level and you made it clear what he or she could expect from you, there will be a certain expectation. When he or she sees an e-mail from you, he or she is going to think, "Oh, this is from Ray. It's probably going to be about copywriting or marketing because I signed up for his copywriting and marketing list."

So, if people get an e-mail from me that has a subject line that says, "This is the neatest copywriting trick I've learned in

10 years," those people on my list are going to respond to that subject line. They're going to open that e-mail, because they know I'm the copywriting guy. That doesn't look like an ad to them, and they want to know what the trick is.

The "C" is curiosity. You want to find a way to elicit some curiosity, such as an incomplete sentence that ends in "…" or with a "?"—something that will compel them to open up the e-mail to find out what you're talking about.

13) Start e-mail with undeniable confirmed truth.

Or, as I like to call it, irrefutable truth. For instance, you may start by giving today's date and/or the time. The e-mails that I send to my list always start with the day's date. If you don't want to do it formally like I do, you could simply make the first line of your e-mail say something like, "Hi Ray, it's me and I'm writing to you on this Tuesday the 13th to tell you that…"

That's starting off with an irrefutable truth. You are writing to me on Tuesday the 13th, and you did write this at 5:27 p.m. As far as I know, that's an irrefutable truth. The reason behind this is a subtle credibility establisher. I learned this from another one of my mentors, Alex Mandossian. It's a very powerful technique.

While it's not necessarily a world-changing action device or response booster, I think it sets up an expectation in the minds of the people reading your e-mails: "He's already started by telling me the truth." There is a subtle ground of credibility that gets laid when you start your e-mail with something that is irrefutably true.

14) Use headline techniques but not headline formatting.

We actually covered this pretty well earlier, so I won't belabor this point. I'll just say again, the less your e-mail looks like an ad, the better.

15) Put the main benefit in the lead with a link.

What is the lead in an e-mail? It's going to be the first sentence or two, possibly the first paragraph or two, where you establish what the e-mail is about.

The lead for your e-mail is going to be the same as the lead for your sales letter. You're doing a couple of things. One, you're setting a tone for what the letter is about, who it's for, why this offer is right for that person, and what he or she needs to do now.

In an e-mail, all that is condensed into a much smaller format. When you have a sales letter, you can develop that message. In fact, that's a good outline for a sales letter. The basic formula for writing any kind of ad, whether it's a sales letter or an e-mail, is essentially the same. It was written many decades ago by advertising greats. You may know it by the acronym AIDA.

AIDA stands for these four words: attention, interest, desire, and action. Any ad or copy you write, if it gets those four emotions from your prospects or readers, it's going to be an effective ad and you're going to get a real lift in sales.

You want to grab their *attention*. You do that with the headline or the subject line.

- You want to stir their *interest*, and you're going to do that in your lead at the beginning of your letter.
- You're going to inflame their *desire* for the solution that your product, service, or offer gives. In an e-mail, this may be a lot more subtle. The burners on this particular stove are turned down pretty low, maybe they're just on warm, so when we talk about that flaming desire, what we really may be doing is eking a little curiosity out of the readers so their desire is to click on this link and see what the e-mail is about.

- Clicking on that link, of course, is the *action*, the most wanted response, we want them to take.

If you think through the AIDA formula each time you're writing any kind of copy and especially for a sales letter, e-mail, or squeeze page, you will do well. When we talk about putting the main benefit in the lead and putting a link there, we want to make sure we run through the AIDA formula in the first sentence or the first paragraph.

A recent study done by the Direct Marketing Association showed that over 80 percent of the clicks from any e-mail promotion came from the first two links in the e-mail. Many savvy marketers know to use multiple links. They may have as many as seven links in one particular promotional e-mail, but if 80 percent of the clicks come from the first two links, that tells me it's important to get a link in there pretty early. If you bury it further down in the e-mail, it may never get a click.

16) Use a PS that summarizes the lead benefit and provides a link.
Now, if that sounds eerily similar to the point we just went over... it is; but it's at the end of the e-mail instead of at the beginning. Just like in your sales letter, the PS quite possibly is the only copy in the e-mail that your prospect actually reads.

Let's walk through the scenario. Your prospects get the e-mail; the subject line is intriguing; they double-click it; it opens up; and immediately their ad radar goes off, even though you're really good. They scroll down to the bottom to see if there's a prize or what this is all about. They see a PS; they scan the PS; and they're gone. Or, a second possible scenario is you provide them with a powerful PS that summarizes your offer and has a link. And maybe, just maybe, they'll click on it to see what it's all about.

There's no guarantee that it's going to work that way, but this is a great opportunity that shouldn't be missed by any marketer. Make sure you have a PS that summarizes the lead benefit and provides a link to your call to action.

17) You want to place a minimum of three links to your call to action in the e-mail body itself.

I've already mentioned that the first two will get most of the clicks. Spreading these three links out evenly is a good idea: beginning, middle, and end. If you can find a way to put more than three links into your e-mail, I recommend you do it.

Don't go crazy, though. Check the spam filter inside your e-mail delivery system, because they only allow a certain number of links. It's based on the volume of the text, the number of words, the spacing, and so forth. It's going to be different with each e-mail, but you want to check it against that spam filter, or spam flag alarm, to make sure you haven't put so many links in the e-mail that it's going to get filtered into somebody's spam basket.

Place a minimum of three links to your call to action. Remember, you have only one call to action. Most likely that will be to have the recipients of your e-mail go take a look at a Web page or some promotion that you have.

18) Send short e-mails that create the Zeigarnik effect.

Your most wanted result with any e-mail is generally to get the prospects to visit a Web page, right? That may be for the purpose of watching a video, to listen to an audio, to opt-in on a squeeze page, or it may be a straight out sales page where you want them to buy something.

Regardless, you probably want them to go to a Web page. The quickest way to make that happen is by employing something called the Zeigarnik effect. Wikipedia says the Zeigarnik effect is the fact that people remember uncompleted or interrupted tasks better than completed ones.

It's named after Russian psychologist Bluma Zeigarnik, who first studied this phenomenon after her professor, Gestalt psychologist Kurt Lewin, noticed that waiters seemed to remember orders only as long as the order was in the process of being served. After it was paid for, they couldn't remember what people ordered.

The Zeigarnik effect is also used in TV shows like *24*. Why do we feel compelled to go back and keep watching *24*? What is it about Jack Bauer? It's because the story is incomplete and it stays on our minds. It's an open loop that our minds have difficulty processing; we want to close that loop.

That's why the cliffhanger every week on that show keeps us coming back. It's why I have two episodes of *24* sitting on my TiVo at home, that I know I must watch before I go on vacation in order to get caught up.

Use the Zeigarnik effect in your short e-mails. Michel Fortin, a colleague and a friend of mine, uses this technique masterfully in his e-mails to his list. He posts most of his content to his blog. Typically, the way he will use the Zeigarnik effect is to simply post a teaser in his e-mail about what's on his blog, so it may read something like this:

"I just posted a little article on my blog about a curious thing called the Zeigarnik effect. You've really got to see how this can raise your response rates." Then there will be the link. That's an open loop that most of us are going to be tempted to close, so we click on the link.

19) Send your e-mails in a specific format.

This is the format I'm going to recommend: plain text, forty-five characters wide with hard carriage returns. By doing this, it forces a line break in the text document—that is, your e-mail. There is software that will do this for you, which is much better and more accurate than doing it by hitting the return key.

I use a piece of software for my Mac called Text Wrangler. For the PC, there is one called Text Editor that performs the same function. You want to use forty-five characters in width because it allows you to control your line breaks. It also provides a lot of white space, which makes your e-mails more readable.

I also recommend you use short sentences and very short paragraphs—if you must write paragraphs in your e-mails. Why? People don't have time. They skim, scan, and scroll. The easier you can make it for them to read the words that you write, the more effective those words will be.

I know text e-mails are not beautiful; they don't have graphics, color, or all those wonderful things we like to put in our e-mails to make them look more professional, but the fact of the matter is the lowest common denominator text e-mails get delivered more readily than html e-mails these days.

In fact, lots of people don't accept html e-mails. You may not know that, but a lot of people actually set their e-mail software to not accept e-mails in any format other than text. Many spam filters will automatically filter out your e-mail if it's sent in html format. I know many marketers use html e-mail, and it works for them. I, however, believe in keeping it as simple as possible. Every e-mail I send is plain text, forty-five characters wide with hard returns.

With that being said, I am considering starting to offer html e-mails but only for those who volunteer. If they sign up for it and express it as a preference, they're probably going to set their software to be able to receive it.

20) Always honor unsubscribe requests.

This simply lets you avoid needless headaches, and it keeps you out of legal trouble. There's a little thing called the Can Spam Act that requires you to unsubscribe people when they ask.

You want to have this happen automatically without you having to deal with it. The best way to do that is to use AWeber.com or 1ShoppingCart.com, also AutoresponsePlus,

MarketersChoice.com, or NewMarketingAutomation.com—any of those private label versions of 1ShoppingCart.

They all have the un-subscription feature built in, so your subscribers can click one link and they're off the list and you don't have to think about it. That is the best way to do it.

If you have multiple e-mail delivery systems on your server and you have your e-mails spread throughout those different accounts, it's very important that you scrub those lists against one another to make sure that if somebody unsubscribes from one of your lists, you take him or her off all your lists to avoid any customer service problems.

21) You don't want to read your complaint e-mails.

Some of you may be reeling with surprise: "What? You don't read complaint e-mails? Don't you care?" I do care. I care too much, and my guess is that you do, too.

Nasty e-mails are nothing but negative energy that will drag you down. If there's a legitimate complaint, I will get involved, but the overwhelming majority of the time, it's a simple matter like unsubscribing. Have someone on your staff do it or have your virtual assistant do it. I have someone who is outsourced support, and I pay him a few dollars a day to go in and check all this stuff for me; he deals with it, and I don't have to worry about it. You can and should do the same.

SUMMARY:

21 Keys to Persuasive Autoresponders and E-mails

1. **Use E-mail Marketing to Build Permission-Based Lists.** Prospects who give you permission to market to them are most likely to buy. Honor (and widen) the circle of permission.

2. **Use a Reputable E-mail Delivery Service.** If your e-mail doesn't get delivered, you won't make any sales; getting it delivered is a full-time job.

3. **Give Web Visitors Reasons to Opt-in.** You must offer some sort of premium to entice visitors to give up their names and e-mail addresses.

4. **Avoid Spam Complaints with Frequent, Consistent Mailings.** Surprising as it sounds, mailing more often can reduce spam complaints.

5. **Use Autoresponders as Robotic Sales Agents.** A sequence of contacts is a powerful way of delivering your sales message.

6. **Create a Sequence That Sells Using Your Sales Letter Copy.** You don't have to start from scratch to write an autoresponder sequence.

7. **Ask for the Sale in Every E-mail.** Treat each e-mail like a miniature sales letter; just be clear what the MWR is for that particular e-mail.

8. **Craft a Powerful Signature File for All E-mails.** This is a powerful action device. Don't forget it.

9. **Use Broadcast E-mails for Promotions.** Broadcasts are great for promotions and launch sequences (time-bound offers).

10. **Know Your Most Wanted Response.** If you don't know it, how can you elicit the desired behavior?

11. **Use Only One MWR.** The confused mind never buys.

12. **Craft Subject Lines Using the PAC Formula.** Write your subject lines so that they are personal, fulfill anticipation, and arouse curiosity.

13. **Start Each E-mail with Undeniable, Confirmed Truth.** For instance, you might start with the date; subtle credibility establisher.

14. **Use Headline Techniques, but Not Headline Formatting.** Avoid making your e-mail look like an ad.

15. **Put the Main Benefit in the Lead, with a Link.** The first paragraph is the lead, and you should have a link to your MWR in that paragraph (or following it).

16. **Use a PS That Summarizes the Lead Benefit and Provides a Link.** Just like in your sales letter, the PS may be the only copy in your e-mail the prospect reads.

17. **Place a Minimum of 3 Links to Your Call to Action in the E-mail Body.** The first two will get most of the clicks.

18. **Send Short E-mails That Create Zeigarnik Effect.** Your MWR is most likely to get the prospect to visit a Web page.

19. **Send E-mails as Plain Text, 45 Characters Wide with Hard Returns.** The lowest common denominator works best.

20. **Always Honor Unsubscribe Requests.** Avoid needless headaches.

21. **Don't Read Complaint E-mails.** And whatever you do, don't get involved in replying; have someone on your staff do it for you.

Chapter 4

How to Write Bullet Points That Virtually Force Your Prospects to Buy

"It's simple. You just take something and do something to it, and then do something else to it. Keep doing this and pretty soon you've got something."

—Jasper Johns

Bullet points are critical to the success of your online sales copy. They make all the difference. Just today, I had a telephone review with a potential client. We were looking through the sales copy for his product.

I immediately identified one of the major problems with that particular copy: no bullet points. Bullet points make your copy easier to read. They make your benefits easier for your readers to digest and personalize. Therein lies the magic of copywriting—getting your readers to imagine themselves enjoying the benefits. That's 90 percent of the work.

I really enjoy the quote at the beginning of this chapter, because in many ways, when we're writing copy, it feels like that's what we're doing. We're taking something—this idea, this copy we're working on—and we just do something to it, and then do something else to it, and pretty soon we've actually got something.

One of the first "somethings" you can do, if you are at a loss as to where to start writing, is to just write … something! I've gone on record as saying I don't believe in writer's block. It's true; I don't believe in it, and I don't suffer from it.

It's because, when I'm stuck, I pick things I *can* write. If I sit down in front of my computer (or with a legal pad, which is sometimes how I write), and I can't think of anything to write and I start feeling that resistance to writing, I just write things I know I can write.

It might be as simple as writing out the guarantee, or maybe even something simpler. It can be writing out the Web site address where the site is going to be, the mailing address or phone number—anything that gets your pen or keyboard moving or gets you dictating, if that's the way you write. Bullet points are a great place to start writing when you're in that stuck place, when that resistance-to-writing feeling sneaks up on you.

Let me give you three things you can do right away to get you started creating great bullet points, even if you feel as though you don't have anything to write at this particular moment.

1) **Start a bullet swipe file**

Remember the "swipe files" from the last chapter? I encourage you to start swipe files whenever you find good copy that you respond to. Start saving the e-mails you receive that catch your interest and make you want to read them. Notice the commonalities of those e-mails that make that happen.

Start saving your snail mail. I'm not talking about the coupons you get from the pizza parlor down the street; I'm talking about promotions you get for magazine and newsletter subscriptions, information products, bigger ticket items that really catch your attention and make you want to open the envelope.

This is good direct-response copy, so every facet of copy deserves its own swipe file. Bullet points are no different. We talked about having a swipe file of great headlines, of great sales letters, and of great e-mails when we covered those subjects. Likewise, I urge you to start a swipe file that focuses specifically on copy that features great bullet points, because it serves as an inspiration.

2) **Write at least 105 bullets of your own**
   Now, I'm going to make this easy for you, because in this chapter, I'm going to give you twenty-one ways to write bullets. All you have to do is write five of each type from the checklist, and you'll have your 105 bullets.

3) **Select your best bullets**
   Pick thirty-five—the top one-third—of those bullets that really sing, the ones that have that kind of poetry that you feel makes a good bullet. After this chapter, you should know what makes a good bullet, so you'll be able to make that judgment intelligently.

Let's talk about the function of bullet points. What are bullet points? What do they do for your copy, and why is it important for you to include them? You've seen bullet points in copy, I'm sure. Especially if you've ever read any of my material. I use a lot of bullet points in my copy.

A bullet point is simply a one- or two-line sentence that's defined by a bullet, a round circle, a checkmark, or perhaps a little box next to it, that sets it apart from the rest of the text. The reason for using bullets in our copy is very simple.

In the first chapter, we discussed the fact that there are three things people never do when first reading your copy. They never read anything at first; they never believe anything at first; and they never do or buy anything at first.

We know they don't read your copy. They skim the copy. They scan through it. They scroll through it. To get them to start reading, we use devices to capture their attention. One of those devices is the headline.

That's what gets their attention initially to get them to read the rest of the ad, copy, or sales page.

The next devices are the subheads, the smaller headlines throughout the copy that telegraph the message of your sales copy.

The third device we use to get people to stop skimming, scanning, and scrolling—and start reading—are bullet points. When they're scanning copy, especially online, readers' eyes are drawn to text surrounded by white space or that looks different from the surrounding copy, such as text set apart by bullet points. Word your bullet points carefully so they're not too wordy, just one or two lines in most cases, so they are quickly digestible.

People can take that in, almost at a glance, and that's where you have the opportunity to start the process of getting your readers to imagine or picture themselves enjoying the benefits that your product or service offers them.

This is the reason we use bullet points in our copy. If you look at successful promotions, off-line or online, almost without fail you'll find that the most successful pieces of copy use lots of bullet points. I don't think that's an accident.

As copywriters, we take note of the clues that are left behind by successful marketing campaigns. Here's a clue: successful promotions use lots of bullet points, and so should we.

For any one piece of sales copy, you should use a minimum of three to five different kinds of bullet points. This is one of the more common rookie mistakes I see—having the same kinds of bullet points stacked up on top of one another.

That becomes monotonous and defeats the purpose of having bullet points in your copy to begin with. If we use the same language to spell out each bullet point, they all start to sound alike. The redundancy reduces the impact we want them to have. You want to mix up the kinds of bullet points you're using in your copy. Break up the monotony with a variety of different approaches.

Always write at least three times as many bullets as you think you will need. That way, you can choose only the best ones for your final copy. Many top copywriters will write many more times that number of bullets. In fact, one of the very top copywriters says he writes seven times as many bullets as he will need for any one given piece of copy.

Think about that. If you decide you're going to need fifty bullets in your copy, that means you're going to write three hundred and fifty bullets to get those fifty. A lot of work? Yes, but does it yield the very best, most response-getting bullets? You bet it does.

So, how many different types of bullet points are there? Well, there are probably hundreds, but my list consists of twenty-one. This list should be comprehensive enough to serve any copywriter's needs.

There's a master bullet that most of these bullets will fall under called the "blind" bullet. What is a blind bullet? A blind bullet is a bullet that tantalizes your reader with a curiosity-inducing statement, yet does not reveal the actual secret behind it, in effect setting up Zeigarnik effect. A void of curiosity that leaves the reader thinking, "I want to know the answer behind that particular bullet." That is one of the things that make bullets so incredibly effective.

There are bullets that are not blind, and I'll refer to those as "naked" bullets. It's not anything saucy; it's simply that we're revealing information in naked bullets, whereas blind bullets are concealing information but hinting in specific ways about that information.

21 Templates for Better Bullet Points

1) The "wrong" bullet.

What do I mean by the "wrong" bullet? The wrong bullet is simply a case where you can contradict a common assumption. You get the reader to state a belief that he or she has, then you say, "Wrong!"

For instance, if you're writing copy for health products, perhaps a nutritional supplement that is designed to reduce high blood pressure, then you might write a bullet that says something like, "Eating lots of salt in your diet is bad for your blood pressure, right? Wrong! We'll explain why when you order our special report. Click here."

You can see why contradicting a commonly held assumption captures the attention of the reader and makes him or her want to know the secret behind the bullet you're writing.

Of course you need to have some factual basis to back up the claim you're making. You can't make a claim that's controversial simply for the sake of controversy, unless you can back the claim up. Assuming that you can, this is a very effective bullet to use.

2) The themed sequence bullet.

This is a case where you are going to spell out, for instance, the seven deadly diet sins, or the three humiliating secrets men don't want women to know.

How might you employ themed sequence bullets in your copy? You might have a paragraph header or a subhead that says, "Seven deadly diet sins that keep you fat!" and underneath have seven bullets, each of which is a blind bullet talking about a deadly diet sin. The first one might be something like, "The three foods you should never eat that are recommended by almost every diet doctor. Eat these foods, and you're sure to stay fat."

The next bullet might be, "Why the time of day you exercise is very important, and why most diet gurus have this information wrong." You see how you would carry out the theme of these particular bullets.

One quick note: just because they are bullet points doesn't mean you have to use actual bullets. Numbers work well, too. If you're spelling out the three humiliating secrets men don't want women to know, then those bullets might be "1-2-3" instead of black circular dots or checkmarks.

3) **The two-step bullet.**

A two-step bullet offers a parenthetical elaboration on the main benefit statement. Sorry if that seems wordy, but it was the most concise way I could write the statement. Let me explain.

This parenthetical statement is the real magnet in the bullet. You know that a parenthetical statement is typically contained in parentheses, so that should make that part easy to understand.

When you have a blind bullet in your copy and you want to heighten the amount of curiosity that is aroused by it, then in parentheses, after your initial bullet statement, make another statement that really makes people think about what it is you're trying to tell them.

For instance, if you're writing a sales letter about a product on networking, one of your bullets might say, "The three top myths about networking." Then in parentheses, you might follow that up by saying, "What never to do with your business card, and why. If you get this wrong, people will walk away and you'll never hear from them again!"

That's a parenthetical statement that heightens the curiosity and enhances or elaborates on the main benefit statement. The implied benefit behind this, of course, is, if you know these myths, you'll be able to avoid these mistakes, and therefore, people will remember you and will call you back.

This is an important point to remember: even when you are talking about mistakes people make, you're talking about benefits—because it's beneficial to learn to avoid them.

4) **The giveaway bullet.**

This one I don't see used very often, especially by new, inexperienced copywriters or marketers, because they don't want to give away their information.

Every now and then in your bullets you should give something away. Give them good information. In fact, I would go so far as to say, give away your best information. Give away your best tricks.

I have built my business giving away my best tricks right up front. In fact, up until recently on the initial page of my copywriting Web site, I was giving away an entire video with my best tricks.

Don't be afraid to give away information, especially information that's self-explanatory in its value. Most marketers are afraid readers will know they've just received the best you have to offer and won't buy anything from you.

Research shows this is not the case. If you can give people a tip or trick that's stunningly good, they are more likely to think, "If that's what they're giving away in their sales promotion, what are they hiding behind the scenes? If the free stuff is this good, what kind of information do I get when I pay them?" You don't want to give away all of your best information, but giveaway bullets, used sparingly, are very effective at credentializing the value of your information.

5) **The reverse hook bullet.**

This is a bullet that presents, first, an interesting fact, and then presents an unexpected benefit that arises from that interesting fact. This is where you have an opportunity to present some of your research. If you find something that's an interesting factoid and you realize it's pertinent to your offer, you can use that as a bullet point.

For instance, let's say you're in the pay-per-click marketing space and you're selling a pay-per-click marketing course that teaches people how to use Google AdWords to drive traffic to their site. One of the challenges in that marketplace is being able to select profitable keywords that generate enough traffic to be able to measure the results that you get from them.

So, you might be able to use a reverse hook bullet that's based on real statistical information. It might say something like, "37.1% of the keywords in your Google AdWords account are not getting enough traffic to give you reliable test data." Now, this is the parenthetical statement, "Here's a simple trick you can use to eliminate these keywords from your ad campaigns forever and save yourself loads of money."

That is a reverse hook bullet. It's an interesting fact that brings an unexpected benefit if you know how to use the information correctly.

6) **The naked benefit bullet.**

This bullet makes a direct benefit claim, but it has got to be supported by some additional facts, or what I call "intrigues," that deepen your reader's interest. You may not be able to come up with a creative way to describe every single benefit you're writing bullets for in your sales copy. You may just need to go ahead and talk directly about the benefit.

For instance, if you are selling a product on how to generate lots of creative ideas, your bullet point—which spells out a naked benefit—might be how to effortlessly generate dramatically different ideas and know instantly if they are worth pursuing.

The benefit is being able to come up with good ideas. You can elaborate a bit and give some other interesting information because you're also offering a technique for evaluating lots of ideas so you can determine which ones are the good ones and which ones need to be weeded out.

7) **The transactional bullet.**

This is very similar to a headline technique that we've already studied. It's simply a proposition that says, "Give me (X), and I'll give you (Y)." It might be something as simple as, "Give me one hour, and I'll teach you how to write effective headlines," or, "Give me three days, and I'll teach you how to buy property with no money down."

It's a transaction. Whenever you're using a transactional bullet, it's often best if you can use it in a case where what you're asking from your readers seems of small consequence in contrast to the benefit you're offering to them.

Let's say, for instance, you are writing copy for a product that offers training in how to use QuickBooks software, and this software teaches users of QuickBooks a simple way to automatically categorize their transactions. In fact, by using your method, they can do in five minutes what used to take them an hour each day to do.

Then you can say something like, "Give me 15 minutes, and I'll teach you how to save 45–55 minutes every day from now on." That's a transactional bullet that makes the transaction seem like a no-brainer for your prospect.

Jay Abraham is famous for teaching "You give me a quarter, and I'll give you a dollar" as the basis for all good salesmanship. I believe that is essentially true.

8) **The if-then bullet.**
This is very similar to number seven. You're giving the prospect something easy for him or her to do or comply with, and you're associating it to a benefit.

This will illustrate how you can use it in a transactional sense. You could write a bullet that says, "If you can spare 10 minutes a day, you can lose five pounds a month." That might allude to a walking program or stair-climbing routine that you can share with people.

You can also use it to show them something that's easy for them to do; and if they can meet that requirement, then they qualify for a greater benefit.

For instance, "If you can send or receive e-mail, then you can learn to make stock trades online in total safety." That's an if-then bullet. You can also use it as a qualifier: "If you are over the age of 50 and have found it difficult to get life insurance, these three simple questions will often get you approved for a life insurance application."

Again, that's a blind bullet, but there's a lot of intrigue there, especially if that's the particular market you're writing for, because that's something they're very interested in learning how to do.

A side note: Even though we're just going through twenty-one bullet types, I hope you can see that you can take each of these bullet types and mix them up and combine them in different ways. You really have hundreds of possible types of bullets you can use, so you're never stuck again for creativity.

You can always come back to this list and ask yourself, "What 'wrong' bullets can I write? What themed sequence bullets could I write? What two-step bullets could I write? What giveaway? What reverse hook? How can I write a naked benefit bullet?"

Some of them may duplicate one another and cross over, but that's okay, because you're expressing the same ideas in different ways. Then you can whittle these down to fine-tune your copy.

So remember when you're going through your bullet writing exercise, don't edit while you're writing—just write. If you sat down and wrote five bullets for each type, then you would have over 100 bullets to choose from for your copy.

9) **The "truth about" bullet.**
This works especially well with any controversial question or issue that is hotly debated. Find an issue where the controversy is well-known in your market. For instance, in the weight loss

market you could write about carbohydrates. As one of your bullet points in your weight loss product copy, you can say, "The truth about carbohydrates - and chances are, it's not what you think it is."

That's a great example of a polarized topic: the role carbohydrates play and how you should manage them in your diet. You can polarize people and catch their interest, whichever side of the issue they may fall upon, simply by using the "truth about" bullet.

10) The "single most" bullet.

You want to use this type of bullet when you have a superior benefit that you can prove. Exercise a little bit of caution with this, because you want to make sure you truly do have the superior benefit and that you really can prove it.

If you have the fastest, easiest, and lowest risk way of lowering your blood pressure, then you should boldly say so: "The single fastest, easiest, and best way of lowering your blood pressure documented and approved by the American Medical Association."

Of course I don't know what that is; I'm making that copy up. (I wish I knew what it was; I could make a fortune!) Just make sure you actually have the "single most" whatever-it-is you're touting. This is an effective way to talk about it. I guarantee you if your product is a superior product in its category, you'll have the opportunity to use at least three or four "single most" bullets within your overall copy.

Give some very careful thought to this. It is a very powerful bullet technique if you don't overuse it.

11) The "how-to" bullet.

This is a simple and very direct approach to writing a bullet. It's the most common type of bullet, and there's a reason why. It's easy to write, and it's effective as all get out, as long as you're a little more creative than the next copywriter is.

Here's what I mean. If you are writing copy for a product that is all about how to grow bigger, better, and more beautiful roses in your garden, you don't want to write a bullet that says, "How to grow better roses." You want a bullet that uses specificity to dimensionalize the benefit you're claiming.

What do I mean by "dimensionalize"? Make it three dimensional. Make it real. Saying "Grow more and better roses" isn't a dimensional type of statement. However, saying "How to grow rose bushes that are literally bursting with mounds of fragrant, colorful, beautiful blooms, with less effort and in less time" dimensionalizes that particular benefit bullet.

Any time you use the how-to bullet, make sure you're using a few more specifics and you're trying to figure out ways to make it more real, more tangible to the reader.

12) The number.

Use this when you have a specific number of techniques or multiple ways of doing a certain thing, multiple reasons why, or multiple reasons why not. Again, this is where you can combine a bullet with other kinds of bullets. You can combine the number bullet with the how-to bullet by simply saying, "Three ways to reduce your heating bill without making you or your family uncomfortable with the temperature of your house."

You're combining a number bullet with a how-to bullet. That's a great way to dimensionalize the how-to bullet. Another way to combine the number bullet with a different type of bullet is to go one step back and look at the "single most" bullet. You could simply say, "The three ways to get 10% better gas mileage from any vehicle with a simple adjustment you can make with a screwdriver."

13) The sneaky bullet.

You've seen this one. You want to use it when you can imply some kind of element of conspiracy. Be careful you don't overuse it, though. There are a few of these bullets I think are overused, especially in the online marketing community. When used effectively, they can be very powerful motivators.

So, what does the sneaky bullet look like when it's in use? Well, it would be something as easy and simple as "The sneaky methods drug companies use to keep you hooked on their products," "Three sneaky tricks used by furnace repairmen to drive up the cost of your maintenance," or "The one sneaky trick almost every auto mechanic uses to inflate your bill and how to avoid being suckered."

You're using the sneaky bullet to imply there is a conspiracy of some kind that your reader is the victim of. This is most effective when you can confirm a suspicion that your reader already has. If you can do so, he or she will immediately be inclined to side with you, because we all love it when other people throw rocks at our enemies and confirm our suspicions. We like being proven right.

14) The "better than" bullet.

This is a great way to get your reader's attention. You want to find something good that you can better. For instance, if you discovered a way to lose weight that was better than the Atkins Diet, you could say, "Better than Atkins."

You'd better be ready to back that up, however. Especially in a health care field, you really have to be careful about complying with FDA regulations.

Consider this a word of caution about using this particular bullet with nutraceuticals, pharmaceuticals, exercise, and any other health-related products. Make sure you're following the directives of the FDA in making those claims.

Let's use a different example. You have a method of doing follow-up marketing that is superior to using e-mail autoresponders. This method of yours nets 100 percent deliverability of your follow-up messages.

Now, each of us knows that e-mail is far from being 100 percent delivered. There are estimates ranging anywhere from 15 to over 50 percent of e-mails not getting delivered to their intended recipient. This isn't spam we're talking about; this is e-mail that people want to receive.

If you could guarantee 100 percent deliverability, you would be able to boldly claim, "Better than e-mail!" Often an effective way to use the "better than" bullet is to simply use a colon. So you might say something like, "Better than e-mail: 100% delivery of your follow-up messages guaranteed!"

15) The simple fact bullet.

When you can't use a blind bullet, use simple facts—but make them interesting. You want to present worst case scenarios to set these particular kinds of bullets up.

For instance, in the health care field there was a study that came out not too long ago that showed people with healthy arteries are susceptible to sudden death because of plaque within their arteries, even though they may not have hardening of the arteries, or arteriosclerosis. Even without a blockage, inflammation within their arteries might cause little pieces of plaque to break off and suddenly block the artery and kill them.

A simple fact bullet, using that information, might say something like, "Healthy people are dying of sudden cardiac arrest," quote the study, then follow up with a comma and say something to this effect: "There are steps you can take to prevent this from happening."

That's a simple fact bullet. It's not much of a blind bullet, but by presenting that simple fact, you can help reinforce the value, the curiosity factor, and the Zeigarnik effect of the other bullets you're using in your copy.

16) The "what" bullet.

I love these bullets because they're the easiest to use. It's a variation of the how-to bullet. The "what" bullet simply answers the question "What?" "What inoculations you need to travel abroad." "What you should avoid touching when you check into a hotel room." "What to do when you're audited by the IRS."

Can you see how easy it is to construct "what" bullets? These bullets are the easiest for you to write.

17) The "what never" bullet.

This is a variation on the "what" bullet. This is the negative form of the "what" bullet. Notice how it frequently plays on the fear factor.

"What never to eat on an airplane." "What never to do immediately after exercising if you want to avoid having a heart attack." "What never to do on a first date if you ever want the person to call you back."

You simply start by stating what one should never do, and then you follow that up with the possible consequences of the reader ignoring this brilliant "what never" advice.

18) The "do you?" bullet.

You use this particular kind of bullet when you believe your readers are doing something that is a mistake. Something that your product, service, or information will help them avoid.

"Do you make these mistakes when filling out your business tax returns?" Then you can use this as a two-step bullet by putting a parenthetical statement after that which says, "If you do, get ready to be audited and you better have your records in order!"

19) The "why" bullet.

It's a simple version of "reason why" copy. "Reason why" copy is a concept that is not often utilized. It is simply the technique of telling people the reasons why they should buy your product or service. Why is your offer superior to another company's offer? Why should they buy now? Why should they buy from you?

"Reason why" is powerful advertising copy, and the "why" bullet is "reason why" copy that hides the reason why.

A good example of "reason why" bullet point copy would be, "The reason why you should always use the lowest octane fuel available at the gas pump, not the highest." That arouses my curiosity. What is the reason behind that? Again, this is a blind bullet, which sets up a Zeigarnik effect.

20) The "secrets of" bullet.

If you have an unusual solution, device, tactic, or method, then you can use this bullet to build curiosity. This is another bullet you need to use with care. You need to use it sparingly. Overuse can eat at your credibility.

If you do know secrets, then using this kind of bullet sparingly helps fuel the fire of curiosity and can be a powerful addition to the bullets that you're using in your copy.

21) The probing question bullet.

Ask a question you are reasonably certain you know the answer to. This is somewhat similar to number eighteen, but eighteen is targeting the readers directly on something that you're pretty sure you know about them personally—either that they're making a certain mistake, that they're engaging in a certain behavior, or they have a certain problem.

This bullet isn't necessarily directed at a mistake they're making or behavior they're engaging in. It can simply be a question about whether, for instance, they have a specific kind of knowledge. "Do you know the seven kinds of deductions the IRS looks for to flag your return for an audit?" "Do you know the three tricks to use at closing to save tens of thousands of dollars on your real estate transactions?" "Do you know the 21 kinds of bullets you can use in your copy that will make it stand superior to other copy and close more sales?" These are all probing question bullet points.

Now, how do you use this list when you're writing copy? You could try what I suggested earlier, simply sitting down and starting with number one, the "wrong" bullet, and writing five or ten "wrong" bullets for your copy.

If you get stuck and you only get three of them, that's okay—just move on. I would use a spiral-bound notebook or a legal pad and just move on to a different page. At the top of the page, write what kind of bullets you're writing. On the second page, you would write the themed sequence bullets and try to write five or ten of those. Again, if you get stuck, don't worry about it—just keep moving.

When you're done with all twenty-one bullet types, you're going to discover that for some of them you've easily got ten bullets and for others you only have five bullets. If you go through all twenty-one with this exercise, you're going to have twenty-one pages: some with ten bullets, some with two, some with five or seven, but you'll end up with many more than 100 bullets, and you can go back through and look at what you've written.

Pick out the ones that you think are outstanding and start migrating those to a different list. You will find you have a variety of bullets to choose from. I would suggest then you simply mix them up and group them on the page. I think it's most effective to break up your bullets into segments of ten or fifteen in a section on your page.

Instead of having fifty bullets in a row, I would break that up into five different lists of ten bullets each, using different bullet types in each of those sections of your copy, breaking that up with different subsections of your copy and paragraphs so the flow stays even. You don't want the flow of your copy to appear jagged.

By not appearing "jagged," I mean you don't want a section that has five big paragraphs followed by a section that is twenty bullets, followed by a section that's one paragraph, followed by a section that's another fifty bullets. You want a more even flow.

For example: two short paragraphs followed by a list of ten bullets, followed by another two short paragraphs, followed by a list of ten bullets. You want the rhythm of your copy to feel consistent.

SUMMARY:
21 Templates for Better Bullet Points

1. **The "Wrong!" Bullet.** When you can contradict a common assumption, use the "wrong!" bullet.

2. **The "Themed Sequence" Bullet.** For instance, "7 Deadly Diet Sins" or "3 Humiliating Secrets Men Don't Want Women to Know."

3. **The "Two-Step" Bullet.** A two-step bullet offers a parenthetical elaboration on the main benefit statement. This parenthetical statement is the real "magnet" in the bullet.

4. **The "Giveaway" Bullet.** Every now and then, "give" them something.

5. **The "Reverse Hook" Bullet.** Interesting fact plus unexpected benefit.

6. **The "Naked Benefit" Bullet.** This bullet makes a direct benefit claim, but it must be supported by some additional facts or intrigues that deepen your reader's interest.

7. **The "Transactional" Bullet.** Simple transaction: "Give me … and I'll give you…"

8. **The "If... Then..." Bullet.** Give the prospect something easy for him or her to do or comply with—and associate it to a benefit.

9. **The "Truth About" Bullet.** Works with any controversial question, point, or issue.

10. **The "Single Most" Bullet.** When you have a provable superior benefit, use this kind of bullet.

11. **The "How-To" Bullet.** Simple and direct approach. This is the most common type of bullet.

12. **The "Number" Bullet.** Use this when you have a specific number of techniques, multiple ways of doing a certain thing, or multiple "reasons why."

13. **The "Sneaky" Bullet.** Use when you can imply an element of conspiracy.

14. **The "Better Than" Bullet.** A great way to get their attention; find something good that you can better.

15. **The "Simple Fact" Bullet.** When you can't use a "blind" bullet, use simple facts but make them interesting. Present "worst case" scenarios to set them up.

16. **The "What" Bullet.** A variation of the "how-to" bullet.

17. **The "What Never" Bullet.** The negative form of the "what" bullet; plays on the "fear factor."

18. **The "Do You?" Bullet.** Use when you think you know they are doing something that is a mistake (which your product avoids).

19. **The "Why" Bullet.** A simple version of "reason why" copy—that keeps the "reason why" hidden.

20. **The "Secrets Of" Bullet.** If you have an unusual solution, device, or tactic, use this bullet to build curiosity.

21. **The "Probing Question" Bullet.** Ask a question you are reasonably certain you know the answer to.

Chapter 5

The Triangular Vise-Grip That Sells More: Irresistible Offers, Risk Reversal, and Powerful Closes

"People get caught up in wonderful, eye-catching pitches, but they don't do enough to close the deal. It's no good if you don't make the sale. Even if your foot is in the door or you bring someone into a conference room, you don't win the deal unless you actually get them to sign on the dotted line."

—Donald Trump

While it's true that proof elements, bullet points, and other elements enhance conversions on your Web site, you could construct a sales letter using nothing more than the following four elements:

➢ Headline
➢ Benefit-rich offer
➢ Convincing risk reversal proposal
➢ Pressure cooker close

That's why you must pay attention to what I call the triad of selling—the offer, the close, and the risk reversal segment. These three elements support the entire structure of your ad. Remember, whatever copy we're writing is an ad whether it's a sales letter, e-mail, landing page, or even an eBay ad—they're all ads.

Here are twenty-one steps to writing irresistible offers, rock-solid risk reversal, and powerful closes:

1) **Make your offer stand alone.**

Think of it this way. If the offer section is the only part of your sales letter that your prospects read, can they make a buying decision? You should be giving them all the information they need to make a buying decision.

You want to construct your offer so it's like a miniature sales letter. It needs a headline, a little deck copy, and a string of benefit-rich bullets that describe what the product is about and exactly what your prospects are going to get when they take advantage of your offer.

Then give them some kind of call to action where they can click and actually order your product or service. So think of it as a miniature sales letter that stands on its own. In fact, if you get stuck, if you get "writer's block" (which I don't believe in), if you're meeting resistance in writing your sales copy, a good place to start is to write your offer. It should be nearly mechanical as you start lifting out the components of your offer. Make it stand alone.

2) **Apply the AIDA formula to your offer.**

What is the AIDA formula? We talked about it in chapter 3, but it's been implicit in everything I've taught you so far. Let me briefly recap the classic advertising formula AIDA.

Every ad should have elements that invoke attention, interest, desire, and then action. Let's think through the structure of a sales letter and overlay the AIDA map on that structure.

How do we get the prospects' *attention*? We get it through the headline and the deck copy. The headline and deck copy persuade them to keep reading our ad. We continue to capture their attention through the body of the sales letter using devices like bullets, subheads, and so forth.

Interest: As we start to evoke images in the minds of the readers and tell a story about how our product or service will benefit them, we're developing their interest. We're showing them how their lives can be transformed by taking advantage of our offer, and that gets their interest.

Once we've progressed to this point, it becomes a fairly simple matter to inflame their *desire* for these outcomes. Remember, the desire is not for the product, because we don't buy products—we buy the end results that products bring us.

If I'm going to spend $1,000 on a suit, it's not because I want a suit with a certain name sewn into the label—it's because I want the feeling that wearing that suit will bring me.

Those feelings might come to me because of the way I feel about wearing a suit with that name on the label. They might come to me because of the way I see myself when I look in the mirror wearing that suit, or those feelings may come to me because by wearing this particular suit I get attention from others that makes me feel attractive, younger, slimmer, or more elegant, whatever the case might be. Always remember that the desire is for the end result. Usually that boils down to an emotional state that we're seeking to evoke in our readers.

Finally, we want to motivate the readers to *action*; and the action we want them to take is to buy our product or service.

So always apply the AIDA formula to your offer. You should be able to overlay AIDA on top of that simple offer box. In fact, you should be using AIDA both outside and inside your offer.

Let me get a little spooky here. I think of AIDA as a kind of fractal formula. If you're familiar at all with the mathematics of fractals, you know that these are patterns that appear the same no matter how far down into the pattern you go or no matter how far back, a micro or macro view.

For instance, if you're looking at a tree and you look at one limb on a branch, you'll notice it looks a lot like the bigger branch itself when you back up. It has little sub-branches, leaves or buds coming off it, just like the big branch. The branch itself actually looks a lot like a little tree, if you back up a little further.

I think the AIDA formula is the same way. It should run as a thread through each section of your letter, so that when you go down to the level of just looking at your offer section, you should be able to identify elements of the AIDA formula.

It may not be as explicit as when we break down the parts of an actual sales letter, but those elements should still be within that offer section. Attention, interest, desire, and action, over and over.

3) Enclose your offer in a box with a dashed border.
You've seen this before—it looks like a coupon you might clip out from a newspaper or magazine. Perhaps you've asked yourself, "Why does this work? Why is it that so many Web sites use this device?" The answer is … I don't really know why it works!

I suspect it's a visual cue that we've linked up in our nervous system that says, "Oh, this is where they're going to talk about what it is I'm supposed to get if I buy their product or service." I think we've probably been trained over the years to think that this is what an offer is supposed to look like.

But, the truth is it doesn't matter why. It simply matters that it is effective. It's another case of not worrying too much about whether we think it's aesthetically pleasing, whether we like the way it looks or not, but realizing that it does work and that effectiveness is what we're after with our sales copy.

4) Use the prospect's positive voice in the offer.
You want to give your prospects the words to say inside their own minds.

I'd like you to take a moment and imagine you're looking at a page on a Web site or in a book. You're reading the words on that page. You look at the page; the light reflects off the page and into your eyes; that signal is sent to your brain; your brain looks at the symbols on the page and interprets them as words; and your inner voice speaks the words in your mind.

Think about the power of that. This is why copy works. You are thinking the thoughts for the reader. If you don't believe that, I'd like you to go back and read what I just described as the process that occurs when you're reading from a page. Isn't it true that you're thinking the thoughts the author told you to think?

The reason this is so powerful when related to offers is that when you write in the prospect's positive voice ("Yes, Ray, I want to take advantage of your Web Copywriting Course. I want to possess the power of turning words into wealth."), you're telling him or her what to think. Even more, I would submit you're thinking the thoughts for him or her using your voice.

The mind is the instrument that your voice is played on. That might sound far out, but I invite you to think about it.

5) **Use aspirational language.**

Invoke your reader's desire. You want to focus on the outcome your reader desires and you want to use language that aspires to that outcome, to gain the emotional state or the sense of being that this outcome will give him or her.

For instance, an aspiration is in the words I just gave you from the offer for Web Copywriting Explained, the copy that says, "Yes, I want to possess the power of turning words into wealth." You're using aspirational language when you describe it.

6) **Use credit card logos and secure site symbols.**

Why is this important? These are symbols that we've been trained to relate to trust, reliability, and stability. By including them, you are reassuring your prospect that your site shares the same qualities.

Remember, the number-one fear prospects have when they come to your selling Web site is that you might rip them off. They're going to give you their credit card information even though they're not certain what you'll do with it.

In most cases, they've never met you. They don't know that much about you, so there is a measure of fear in this process. Everything you can do to remove that fear is vitally important to closing more sales. So use the credit card logos, which are familiar and trusted icons in our society, and include your guarantee. This is all inside the offer box.

We're going to talk more about the guarantee on its own, but now I'm talking about including the guarantee inside the offer box and also the Better Business Bureau logo if you are authorized to use it. I recommend you become authorized to use it.

I am part of a group that is sharing information about results from various marketing tests we've been doing. One of the mastermind group members related the results he had when he added the BBB logo to his Web site.

It was so astounding, his conversions actually tripled! That's when I made my decision to join the BBB. It's an inconsequential investment—about $600 a year to be a member—and there's a process of approval you have to go through.

Having just gone through it myself, I will tell you it's not that difficult. Sometimes I'm asked if the process to become a BBB member is real. I can say unequivocally yes. They really do check you out. That's why consumers are reassured by it. Once you go through the approval process and pay your dues for the year, then you're entitled to use their logo. I strongly recommend you join the BBB and use their logo on your Web site.

7) **Use both an order button and a text link.**

I recommend you use an html button and not a graphic order button, although there are very smart marketers and good arguments on both sides of the debate.

I prefer the html order button for one simple reason. It works and looks right in all browsers, which may or may not be the case for a graphic icon or button. So why do I recommend you use both? It's always best to assume that your user or reader doesn't really know with 100 percent certainty what to do next.

If your prospects have been conditioned to think they're supposed to click on the button, they may be confused by the link, or vice versa. Why not give them both options, so no matter what they choose to do, they end up at your order process page? I believe giving them every opportunity to order is the best option of all.

I also make the graphic of the credit cards into a live buying link as well, because sometimes you'll find people will click on those graphic credit card representations to buy.

How do I track what people are clicking on? If you want to do some testing on your own, you can track where people are clicking their mouse, so you can know which elements are converting best for you. If you do this, you could eliminate some of the dead weight and add more of the high converters into your copy. My recommendation is a site called CrazyEgg.com.

8) **Do not sleepwalk through the guarantee.**

The guarantee is also known as the risk reversal section of your copy. Why do we call it risk reversal? As we said earlier, the biggest fear prospects have when they come to your Web site is the fear that you are going to rip them off.

Job one is convincing them of your credibility, reliability, and stability, so they understand that you're not going to rip them off. The next fear they have is that they're going to be persuaded to buy your offer and it's not going to be exactly right for them.

You want to reassure them—as much as possible—that the decision they're making is the right decision and that they cannot make a mistake. That's what the risk reversal section is all about. This is where you make it clear to them you're taking the risk off their shoulders and placing it squarely on your own shoulders.

If you don't believe this is true, I'd like you to think about something: If someone orders your product or service and he or she is not satisfied with it and asks for a refund, you have to ship the refund back to him or her and he or she has to ship the product back to you. Who was the loser in the transaction? If you require your buyer to pay all the shipping and so forth, you might think you haven't really lost anything … but you have.

At the very least, you've lost the time and energy it took to fulfill the order, to deal with the refund request, to make the refund, and then to restock your item. Haven't you then taken the risk away from your buyer and taken it upon yourself?

By offering a guarantee, aren't you really saying, "I'm willing to stand by the quality of my product or service, and I'm so confident of the quality of that product or service that I'm willing to take the risk of giving you a guarantee even though you might choose to send my product back"?

I choose to think of it like this: Even though I know my product is top quality and delivers more than I promise in my sales letters and communications, I know that some people—for whatever reason—will choose to not honor our transaction and will request a refund (perhaps even after copying the material I've sent them!). They may even order my product, never open it, and then just before the guarantee period is ending, send it back to me quickly. I feel they have dishonored our transaction by not opening the material, looking at it, or reviewing it, or by deciding ahead of time that they were just going to order the material, copy it, and send me back the information.

Even though I believe that kind of behavior is dishonorable, I'm still willing to honor the guarantee, because the truth is, if you do your job in your sales copy and you do your job delivering your product or service, the number of people who will rip you off by requesting a refund is very small. Sadly, it happens. It's just a part of doing business.

There are techniques you can use to reduce the number of people who will ask for those refunds. I really want you to get—deep in your bones—the fact that risk reversal is exactly what it says. It's not some semantic trick of language; it truly is reversal of risk.

Don't sleepwalk through writing your risk reversal or guarantee section. Don't just write "100% money back guarantee." I think you should offer that, but it's important to give it an extra dimension. Describe your guarantee in fresh unique ways. We're going to look at that in some of our case studies later on in this chapter.

9) Put your risk reversal inside a certificate.

This creates credibility, and it increases conversions. Putting something in certificate form lends it credibility. I know by using testing methodology that we can prove putting the risk reversal or guarantee inside a certificate increases conversions. It works.

10) Keep selling, especially in the risk reversal section.

This is a perfect place to restate the benefits of your offer. People are going to look at your guarantee. It's quite possible it'll be one of the few things they actually read on your page before making a buying decision.

It's an opportunity for you to restate your benefits. How do you do this? It's a very simple technique. Just describe the benefits in your guarantee or risk reversal language.

Let me give you an example. "Order my e-book, read every page. If you're not delighted with the results, if in fact you don't lose at least 30 pounds in 30 days, find it easy to eat the right foods without feeling hungry or deprived, know in an instant what you're supposed to eat without ever having to refer to a calorie chart or point system, then I refuse to keep your money."

See what I did? Didn't I just restate the benefits in that sentence, which was part of a guarantee? You can do the same, and you should. Keep selling even in your guarantee section.

11) **Use 100 percent money back language, but don't rely on that to convey the message of your guarantee.**
Use active language to dimensionalize your guarantee. I've already described this, but pay attention to this step carefully.

I do believe you should include the 100 percent money back guarantee language. Some people simply look for that phrase as their assurance that there are no tricks involved in your guarantee. For some, it's important that you use that specific language in your guarantee. Use it, but don't make that the only guarantee you offer; be more descriptive.

12) **Add audio to your risk reversal section.**
You want to make your risk reversal or guarantee personal, persuasive, and passionate. One of the best ways you can do that is by using the human voice, especially if your personality is part of your marketing.

Use a service like Audio Generator, for instance. You can just read the actual risk reversal language from the certificate itself. Place your picture with an audio button underneath. The reader presses the button and hears your voice coming out of the guarantee section saying:

"Hi, this is Ray Edwards, and I just want to reassure you our policy is you must be satisfied in every way with the product or service you're ordering or we will send you 100 percent of your money back. Not only will we send it back, we will rush it to you overnight FedEx check. I want you to know with full assurance that we absolutely refuse to keep your money if you don't believe you have more than your value's worth."

13) Use your signature in the risk reversal section.

It increases conversions. Why? If it's signed, we feel like it's a deal; it's official; it's a contract. If I put my signature on something, I'm making a statement that says I identify with this guarantee, with this product, or with this risk reversal. I identify myself with it; my word is my bond, and here's my signature to prove it. In our society this is true.

Some people are concerned about using their actual signature online. There are a number of solutions to that problem. First, you can have someone else sign so the signature would be distinct from your own. Then, there would never be a problem with forgery. You can also use handwriting software that generates handwritten text that appears to be real but isn't your real signature.

I would suggest you not just use the handwritten fonts that you have in MS Word. They're not very convincing. People have seen them before, and they will know that's not your signature. When people look for a signature, they want to see a real signature from a real person.

So if you're going to use a software or handwriting font solution, then I recommend you invest in a good one. For instance, there is a manufacturer's software called V-Letter, which I believe you can find at Vletter.com. This software generates cursive, script, handwriting fonts and signatures, and it looks absolutely real. And, they're a member of the Better Business Bureau program! Use your signature and sign the deal, which leads to ...

14) Use a handwritten guarantee.

If a signature works, a handwritten guarantee often works even better. Handwritten guarantees have been shown time and again to authenticate the guarantee in the reader's mind and increase conversion dramatically.

If you're going to use a handwritten guarantee, you want to make sure that it's short, powerful, and most important, legible. Nothing is worse than a guarantee where the handwriting is so bad you can't read it. Make sure it's legible, because this can be a very powerful technique.

15) The close happens at the order form.

This is where you're asking for the sale, the order. You're taking their money and giving them the product in exchange. There is a little bit of confusion sometimes about this because most marketers have the close contained in the offer. I look at them as two distinctly different items.

The offer portion of your sales letter, when clicked, leads to the payment page or order page. In my model of online selling, that page includes copy at the top that probably duplicates a lot of the copy you just saw in the offer box in the sales letter.

The difference is the entry blanks to put in your name and credit card information are at the bottom of this page. In large part, this has been dictated by the methods we use to take payments online, shopping cart software and the like.

Some systems allow you to take the credit card information right on the sales letter itself. I haven't done any tests to determine whether that's more effective than clicking on an offer section and being led to an order page. I do know having the reader click on the offer section of a sales letter to be taken to the order page works very well, when done correctly.

I hope I'm clarifying where the actual close takes place: it's on the order page. The order page will consist of a congratulatory headline that affirms the decision the buyer has just made. This is where we take his or her credit card information. He or she is going to press the submit button and make the order—that's the close.

16) Use all the tools that are available to you at the close.

That means you want a headline on the order page just as I described: one that's affirmative, congratulatory, and lets them know they've made the right decision. You want to recap all the major benefits, probably the same ones you had listed in your offer box on the sales letter page. Restate your guarantee or your risk reversal.

You want to use urgency, scarcity, and reward. Urgency and scarcity can be accomplished by setting limits. Set a time limit: "You must order by Friday at 5:00"; or a numerical limit: "We only have 13 of these kits available. You must order before they're all gone"; or a date limit based on a sale's expiration. If you can introduce some urgency into the selling process ethically and honestly, then you should do it.

For a reward, you might offer, "For the next 10 people who order this product, we will also give you a special report on …" or "… we'll give you a second gizmo" or whatever the appropriate bonus offer might be. That rewards fast action. Make sure you're offering a limited number or a limited time on your bonus items, and make certain it's all honest and ethical.

Nothing can hurt your credibility more than if you say, "We will offer this bonus only until Friday at 12:00 noon!" Then your reader comes back Friday at 1:00 p.m. to see if you were lying or not and discovers that, in fact, you were lying. In fact, you've changed the date on the Web site using a sneaky little script.

Don't resort to those kinds of tricks. Take the time and effort to make your promotions real, honest, and ethical. You will be rewarded in return.

17) Tell your reader what to do to close the deal.

This is where you need to be as specific as possible. In fact, you might even feel as though you're writing to a third grader. You're going to use language like this: "Okay, now's the time to type in your name and your address, double-check that the information is correct, then type in your credit card number and click on the 'Buy now' button."

You want to be just that specific in your instructions. If you can give these instructions in audio or video, that's even better.

18) You want to reassure and praise your readers.

Everyone craves affirmation. Give them what they want. If you've created a truly useful product or service that makes a difference in the lives of buyers, you should have no shame in saying, "I'm so proud of you for making this decision to buy my product or service, and I'm so excited about the difference it's going to make in your life. I can't wait to hear your success story, and I do hope you'll share it with me. Here's what you should do right now, type in your name, address, and credit card information and click the button that says 'Buy now,' so I can rush your items to you right away."

Reassure and praise your reader for the good decision he or she made.

19) Explain what's going to happen.

Tell them exactly what's going to happen when they press the "Submit" or "Buy now" button. This is a question your reader is wondering about. "When I click on this, am I going to get a printable receipt? Am I going to be taken to a download page? What's going to happen when I click that button?"

The best way to reassure them is to tell them what's going to happen or even show them if you can make a screen capture video that shows exactly what's going to happen. Have a message or arrow pointing to the video that says, "Click here to watch a video about what happens next."

You could have audio that plays, saying, "When you click the 'Buy now' button, you'll be taken to a page where you can immediately download your items, and you can also print out your receipt and proof of purchase on the next page. Go ahead and click the 'Buy now' button now."

20) Maintain the look and feel of your Web site.

Your order form should look exactly like your Web site. In many cases, the order form will be hosted somewhere other than your own server. Usually, it will be hosted through the shopping cart system.

There is a problem, however, when the order page looks entirely different from your actual Web site. Unconsciously, your prospects will feel there's a disconnect between what you're telling them and what you're selling them.

You want to make the transition seamless. When people enroll in my Web Copywriting Explained course, they probably don't even notice when they go from clicking on the order button to getting to the download or access page that they actually switch servers two times. That's by design. We made sure the pages look exactly the same when you make that transition. You should do the same—keep the look and feel identical.

There is a phenomenon called the unconscious parallel association. This simply means your readers are noticing the look and feel of your Web site. If it's inconsistent, they feel that you are inconsistent—that your business is inconsistent.

How do we feel about people in our lives who are not consistent? How do you feel about a business or institution that treats you in an inconsistent manner? Don't you feel you can't rely on them, that you can't trust them to behave in a certain way? You don't want your readers, prospects, or buyers to feel that way about you, so don't give them a reason to.

21) **Test your order form.**

Sometimes it's the simplest things that can trip up your shopping cart system. If you haven't tested it before your Web visitors use it, you could potentially be in for some embarrassing occurrences.

Order your own product. If it's an expensive product and you want to minimize your processing expense, set it to zero dollars or one dollar and make multiple orders. Try to break your order form; try to put in erroneous information. Think about what your prospects might do on your order page that could possibly trip up your system and then do those things and see what happens.

It's better if you know in advance, rather than discover it when you get that complaint call from an unhappy buyer or when you watch sales trickle through your fingers because your order form didn't work properly.

Many times I find that clients and companies don't even realize they're losing orders. This is where many orders are lost, at the actual order page in the shopping cart. Make sure you have a backup plan. What's going to happen if the customer's credit card is declined or the transaction doesn't go through? Do you call him or her? Is the customer taken to a different Web page? Think about what happens next in that process and plan for it. Recover from declined cards and abandoned shopping carts and you will increase sales.

SUMMARY:
21 Steps to Irresistible Offers, Rock-Solid Risk Reversal, and Powerful Closes

1. **Make Your Offer "Stand Alone."** If the offer section is the only part your prospect reads—can he or she make a buying decision?

2. **Apply the AIDA Formula to Your Offer.** Invoke attention, interest, desire, and a call to action.

3. **Enclose Your Offer in a Box with a Dashed Border.** Make it look like a coupon you might clip from a newspaper.

4. **Use the Prospect's Positive Voice in the Offer.** Give the prospect the words to say inside his or her own mind.

5. **Use Aspirational Language.** Focus on the outcome your reader desires.

6. **Use Credit Card Logos and Secure Site Symbols.** Reassure your prospect with these familiar icons; also include your guarantee and the BBB logo (if you are authorized to do so).

7. **Use an Order Button AND a Text Link.** Make it easy and obvious how you wish the reader to proceed.

8. **Do Not Sleepwalk Through the Guarantee.** This is the biggest mistake made with the risk reversal section.

9. **Put Your Risk Reversal Inside a Certificate.** This creates credibility and increases conversions.

10. **Keep Selling—Especially in the Risk Reversal Section.** State your benefits as part of the guarantee.

11. **Use "100% Money-Back," but Don't Rely on It.** Use active language to dimensionalize your guarantee.

12. **Add Audio to Your Risk Reversal Section.** Make it personal, persuasive, and passionate.

13. **Use Your Signature in the Risk Reversal Section.** Increases conversions.

14. **Use a Handwritten Guarantee.** Handwritten guarantees can work very well when *you* are the product.

15. **The Close Happens at the Order Form.** Until they press "Submit," you don't have an order.

16. **Use All Available Tools at the Close.** Benefits, guarantee, audio, video, urgency, scarcity, and reward.

17. **Tell Your Reader What to Do to Close the Deal.** Be as specific as possible.

18. **Reassure and Praise Your Reader.** Everyone craves affirmation; give it to them.

19. **Explain What's Going to Happen.** Tell them exactly what will happen when they press "Submit."

20. **Maintain Look and Feel.** Your order form should look like your Web site.

21. **Test Your Order Form!** Try to "break" it. Have a backup plan. Recover from "declines" and "abandons"; increase sales.

Chapter 6

The Most Explosive Tactics for Making More Sales, More Often, with Less Human Effort Than You Ever Dreamed Possible

"Words mean more than what is set down on paper. It takes the human voice to infuse them with deeper meaning."

—Maya Angelou

Audio and video are the hottest things on Web pages today. Because of their nature, you might think that audio and video will kill online copywriting. Will this be the end of sales letters? My answer is an emphatic no. A century ago, people thought that radio—and later, TV—were going to be the death of newspapers and books, too.

In this chapter, we're going to talk about how to write copy for audio and video and the proper usage of them in your online marketing efforts.

21 Tips for Better Audio & Video Copy

1) **Use audio and video where appropriate.**

   Don't just throw audio and video on your page because it's the latest thing. It can be very useful, but sometimes we get so caught up in the latest industry tricks that we don't make certain we have a reason for those tricks. Not every site needs to have audio or video—you must analyze the need for them on your page.

I recommend you use audio on a squeeze page regardless of the service or product. Do you want to use video on a squeeze page? Not always. The same thing applies to a sales page.

The coolest video is still not going to sell lousy offers. Still, I think anything you can do to enhance your site, make it appear to be more professional than other sites in your industry, gives you a strategic advantage.

2) **Use proven technology to deliver your media.**
Using buggy software or sluggish servers to deliver your audio, in order to save a few bucks, is a big mistake. If your audio or video isn't being delivered in a smooth, streaming fashion, if people can't download it, it will undermine your efforts. Make sure you aren't cutting off your nose to spite your face.

Many people decide they don't want to pay for AudioGenerator or InstantVideoGenerator every month, so they will host their own audio or video. Almost invariably it's a problem. Go look at any of my Web sites. You will see I use AudioGenerator or InstantVideoGenerator to deliver nearly all my materials.

I will tell you during the launch of Web Copywriting Explained, I was hosting my own video on my server and it caused a lot of problems. The short answer to this is NewAudioMarketing.com or NewVideoMarketing.com. Always make it a practice to use proven technologies.

3) **Technology is a means to an end.**
Don't get caught up in the technology—it's just a tool. I have a friend who was enthralled by a new Web video course that involved a really cool trick. The trick involved having your full

body walking out from behind the headline and walking across in front of the headline, talking. It's a very nifty trick.

My friend got so caught up in learning how to do this, he was spending hours working on this. I asked him, "Why are you so caught up in this? What are you going to do with it?" His answer to me was, "I don't know. I just think it's cool."

Most of us should be spending our time on revenue-generating materials, rather than on learning cool tricks with technology. Maybe there is a reason you want to spend the time learning how to do that kind of thing, but for most of us, we could be spending our time better.

Earl Nightingale used to talk about the difference between successful people and people who were failures. His basic premise was: successful people do the things that failures don't like to do. He summed it up this way: "There are two kinds of activities. There are goal achieving activities and there are tension relieving activities."

A lot of times, learning new fun technology is a tension-relieving activity. Technology is a means to an end; don't let it chew up your goal-achieving, revenue-generating work time.

4) **Use audio in e-mails.**

This is where we start getting into the nitty-gritty of learning where and how to use audio or video.

The first thing I would tell you is to use audio in e-mails. You may know this as audio postcards. This is, as far as I know, the term that was invented by Alex Mandossian, the chief instructor and creator of Teleseminar Secrets. Audio postcards are e-mails with a link to the audio.

The simplest way you can put this to work in your e-mail is to put a link at the top of your e-mail that says something like, "Listen to this e-mail instead of reading it."

Then put a link to your audio postcard, which you created inside AudioGenerator. There are other tools, but AudioGenerator is so easy to use. I'm an audio nut. I worked in the radio business for over a quarter of a century. I know about audio. I know about recording gear. I certainly know about computers, technology, the Internet, and all of that.

It's not hard for me to set up my own audio and make my own audio buttons on my own server. I use AudioGenerator because it's so simple and easy; it doesn't get in the way of my getting things done in a quick and efficient fashion. That includes using audio in e-mails by making audio postcards. This is proven to get you more response from your e-mails. Use audio in your e-mails.

5) Use auto-play audio on squeeze pages.

Imagine: someone comes to visit your squeeze page, and the audio starts playing immediately. "Hi, this is Ray Edwards. Welcome to this site. I'm so glad you're here. I've got a free report that you absolutely must download if you want to learn the secrets to overcoming your arthritis pain once and for all. Just put in your name and e-mail address below to get this free report."

The question that always comes up is, "Ray, isn't that going to annoy people? Doesn't that bug people? Aren't there going to be people who are at work that don't want to hear that kind of message just blaring out of their computer?"

The answer is yes, it will annoy people. Yes, it will bug some people, but not the majority of people. It has been proven time and time again to boost the number of opt-ins that you will get.

So if you have, for example, a hundred visitors to your Web page and you're getting twenty opt-ins, if you just add the auto-play audio, you can boost that to thirty or forty opt-ins. You could quite literally, just by adding the right audio, double the conversions that you get for opt-ins to your list.

Would you prefer to annoy a few people and double your opt-ins, or would you rather keep that troublesome, yet smaller, group of rabble-rousers happy, but not get as many opt-ins as you might possibly have gotten?

I think the answer is obvious. Most of us are going to say, "I don't want to upset anybody, but if I get double the opt-ins, I really should have audio on that page." That's why I recommend you do it.

6) **Use push-to-play audio on sales pages.**
This means you have audio buttons on your sales letter page that must be pressed in order for the viewer to hear the audio. You don't want to put an automatically playing audio on the actual sales page itself. Your goal is to get people to read the sales page.

If you have auto-play audio, a lot of times people will shut off the audio the quickest way they know how, which is to click over to another Web page. Now you've lost them. That's the reason for not putting automatically playing audio on your sales page.

Where should you put your push-to-play audio buttons on your sales page? I recommend that you have them in at least three places. Those places are in your headline, in your guarantee, and in your actual offer section.

Your readers may or may not choose to listen to the audio that you provide in those places, and that's okay. If they're audio-oriented people, they will press the button and they will appreciate the fact that you actually put the audio there.

7) **Push-to-play audio on key sections of the copy.**
This is in addition to the three sections I just mentioned. This is especially useful if you have sections of your copy that are perhaps harder to understand, or are key to making the sale,

or if you want to try to be on the cutting edge. If any of these apply, I definitely recommend that you test this.

You could, in fact, create an entire audio version of your sales letter simply by putting an audio button under each subhead in your sales letter.

One thing that I want you to keep in mind when you're placing audio buttons, for instance, in your guarantee or in your offer section or when you are putting audio buttons in each major section of your sales letter is that it does not replace the copy. It complements the copy; it might even duplicate the copy; but you still want to have text on the screen. Why is that?

Some people keep their speakers turned off; some people cannot hear or have hearing challenges, so you want them to be able to read what you have to say. Some people are just more visually oriented than they are auditory, so you want to influence them in the learning modality that they're most responsive to.

Audio doesn't replace copy; it enhances, compliments, or duplicates copy.

8) Auto-play audio on order pages boosts conversions.
Shopping cart abandonment is one of the top reasons you lose sales. People come to your Web site; they go through your squeeze page; they get on your list; they look at your sales letter; they read your sales letter; they read the offer; and they click on the button that says, "Order now." They are taken to a shopping cart page and something terrible happens.

Nothing. They look at the page, and for whatever reason, they decide to go somewhere else. They give up. In some cases, they give up before they do anything. Sometimes it's because they reach an error message, and then they're gone. Regardless, you've lost the sale. It's called "shopping cart abandonment."

Millions of dollars have been spent researching how to minimize this problem.

From previous chapters, you know you need to have sales copy on your shopping cart page that looks and feels like your Web site, that reiterates all the benefits of your offer, restates your guarantee, and speaks to them in affirmative, aspirational language.

If you will simply add auto-play audio to your order page, you can increase conversions and reduce shopping cart abandonment. It should say something like this: "Hi there. It's Ray Edwards. I just want to congratulate you on making a great decision. You just decided to claim your spot in Web Copywriting Explained, where you will go through all eight modules and learn my entire system for writing copy that sells more of your products or services. Here's what you need to do now." Then you walk them through the process of placing their order and tell them how they will receive access to the product that they ordered.

Your audio praises the buyer for making a good decision, reiterates the benefits of your product, and tells the buyer what to do next. It will help eliminate some of the common errors that occur on the shopping cart page. By simply asking your buyer to double-check his or her information, you help eliminate frustration for your buyer and lost sales for you.

9) **Auto-play audio on thank-you pages suppresses refunds.**
Doing this will reduce the number of refund requests you receive, and it will also reduce the number of customer service requests you get. As you become more successful, as you sell more units of your product or service, you will see more customer service requests, as well.

You will quickly figure out the most common customer service questions, so answer them in your thank-you page audio. Perhaps it would sound something like this: "Success! Your transaction was processed. Here is your download page.

Please note the links below. You're going to be receiving a confirmation e-mail that will serve as your receipt. I also would like to take a few minutes to answer some of the most frequently asked questions..." and then you're off to the races.

By the way, I would also encourage people to bookmark the download page, so that they can easily get back to it. It will help keep them from getting frustrated and cuts down on customer service requests.

10) Write your scripts carefully.

Spend as much time on this as you do on any other copy you use. The ad-lib copy is often the most difficult to deliver properly. I spent over twenty-five years in the radio business. For many years I did about four hours of it per day. Even then it was difficult. Don't expect it to be any different for you. Write out your audio/video copy very carefully. Don't try to wing it. It won't be as effective, nor as good as it could be. You will miss out on opt-ins and sales.

11) Deliver your scripts naturally.

There is an art to reading copy that sounds like your own words being spoken for the very first time. In fact, that is a skill that those involved in drama must learn. And in time, most people can learn how to do this. But not everyone.

If you sound like you are just reading it, pay someone to do your voice-over work. Find someone who can make it sound like he or she is just speaking naturally. If you can't find voices to do this for you, I would suggest Voices.com.

12) Make your audio and video high quality.

This flies in the face of advice you're getting from many sources in the online marketing world. Perhaps this comes from my years working in the professional audio field. Use high-quality microphones. Get the highest quality sound you can get. Use good lighting, if you're shooting video.

Your audio/video leaves a certain impression about you. What impression will that be if you're not using the best quality product that you can?

Now we're going to get into some specifics about writing your script.

13) Script Key #1: Know your MWR.

If you don't know what your most wanted result is, your response rates will suffer. If you don't know what you're asking for, how can you possibly expect to get it? Is it to get them to opt-in? To watch a video? To get a sale?

Before you start writing copy, decide what your most wanted result is. Know it in advance.

14) Script Key #2: Structure your copy strategically.

This is a big problem in online marketing. People either wing it—or worse—they copy what other amateurs are doing. There are some very successful online marketers who are clearly amateurs when it comes to audio/video.

They could really skyrocket their sales if they would just improve this one part of their marketing. Don't learn from other amateurs; learn from the professionals. Learn from direct-response radio advertising.

Armand Morin and Alex Mandossian and Jeff Walker are three online marketers who are all doing audio and video well— but they all three do it differently. Study what they are doing.

15) Script Key #3: Keep copy short.

Shorter copy is better. Short sentences convey ideas quickly. They're easy to digest. It's easy to process the information. It's easy to follow the conversation.

See what I did? I used short sentences. Enough said.

16) **Script Key #4: Use short words and sentences.**

Keeping words and sentences short will make your copy more effective. This is different from Script Key #3—don't put a five-minute audio on your squeeze page. You only have a short amount of time; keep it short.

This key means if you have sixty seconds on your squeeze page audio, don't make it all one sentence. Break it up.

17) **Script Key #5: Make your call to action clear.**

This is another huge mistake—usually not on squeeze page audio, generally on the sales page audio. They don't remember that there is a call to action.

Make it clear; don't leave them wondering what to do next.

18) **Use video when there's a reason to do so.**

I'm going to encourage you to avoid the "everyone else is doing it" mindset. Just because everyone else is using video on their Web pages, it doesn't mean it's a good choice for you.

If you are wanting to demonstrate something and the best and most exciting way to do that is through video, then that would be good. Video testimonials for a high ticket item is a good choice as well.

Now, before you even ask, I'm going to answer your question. I don't care what you look like; people like to communicate with real people. First of all, you're probably better looking than you think you are. Secondly, there is nothing more real than a real-looking person, with real "imperfections."

In America, most people that we see in the media are the genetic abnormalities. The rest of us are normal. It doesn't matter. Get over yourself. You are a real person, and your real personality will come through. People respond to real people who are passionate about what they're selling.

This applies to how you think you sound, as well, by the way. Don't worry about that. Just be yourself.

19) Make video clear, but not "slick."

It's important that your video is clear and well lit. You also want high-quality sound. You don't want it to seem like a Hollywood commercial.

Most people equate that with fake. I would urge you to overcome the inclination to make your videos slick.

20) Use close-mic sound in your video.

Close-mic means that the microphone is close to the mouth of the person speaking. Generally, that is accomplished by using a lavaliere mic. You have seen a speaker wearing a microphone clipped to his or her tie or collar. That's called a lavaliere microphone.

This will make all the difference when you're shooting video. If you have superior sound, other things, even your picture, could be inferior and you will still have a good video.

21) Test ruthlessly.

This is at least as important with your audio and video as it is with the text of your sales copy. Definitely test. Test everything. Test often.

Test different videos and audio. Test no video versus video. Test no audio versus audio. Test the length, the duration, and if you can afford to do this, test different voices. There are an endless number of things you can test when it comes to your video and audio. At the very least, test with and without to see which converts better.

SUMMARY:
Audio and Video Copy Explained

1. **Use Audio and Video Where Appropriate.** Avoid using these media simply because you can.

2. **Use Proven Technology to Deliver Your Media.** Don't let buggy, sluggish servers undermine your efforts.

3. **Technology Is a Means to an End.** Avoid getting caught up in your technology; it's only a tool.

4. **Use Audio in E-mails.** Put a link at the top of e-mails that says, "Listen to this e-mail"—proven to boost conversions.

5. **Use Auto-play Audio on "Squeeze Pages."** Yes, it annoys people. Yes, it increases sign-ups to your list.

6. **Use Push-to-Play Audio on Sales Pages.** Definitely have at least three audio buttons on your sales pages: headline, guarantee, and offer.

7. **Use Push-to-Play Audio on Key Sections of Copy.** This is especially useful for sections that are hard to understand or key to making the sale.

8. **Auto-Play Audio on Order Pages Boosts Conversions.** Prevent "shopping cart abandonment" by telling readers what to do next.

9. **Auto-Play Audio on Thank-You Pages Suppresses Refunds.** Reassure buyers; explain what they should do now.

10. **Write Your Scripts Carefully.** Spend as much time on this as you do on any of your other copy.

11. **Deliver Your Scripts Naturally.** Either deliver your copy so that it does not sound as if you're "reading it" or pay someone to do it for you.

12. **Make Your Audio and Video High Quality.** Quality counts. Use good microphones, lights, etc.

13. **Script Key #1: Know Your MWR.** If you don't know your most wanted result, your response rates will suffer.

14. **Script Key #2: Structure Your Copy Strategically.** Use my audio/video templates to write your copy.

15. **Script Key #3: Keep Copy Short.** Shorter copy is better.

16. **Script Key #4: Use Short Words and Sentences.** Keeping words and sentences short will make your copy more effective.

17. **Script Key #5: Make Your Call to Action Clear.** Never let people wonder what to do next.

18. **Use Video When There's a Reason.** Be careful of "everyone else is doing it" syndrome.

19. **Make Video Clear but Not "Slick."** It's important that your video be clear, well lighted, with high-quality sound … without seeming too "slick."

20. **Use Close-Mic Sound in Your Video.** Invest in a lavaliere mic or good uni-directional mic so your sound is superior. The sound in your video is more important than the images!

21. **Test Ruthlessly.** At least as important with your audio and video as with your text.

Chapter 7

The Secret Way to Attract a Flood of Web site Visitors as Easily as Turning on a Water Spigot

"Promise, large promise, is the soul of an advertisement."
—Samuel Johnson

In my career, I have had a behind-the-scenes look at the business practices, procedures, tools, and actions of some top Internet marketers like Alex Mandossian, Frank Kern, Joel Comm, Willy Crawford, Brad and Matt Callen, and many others whose names you're familiar with.

I'm not going to reveal to you any of their proprietary information, secrets, or anything that would compromise their competitive advantage in the marketplace.

I am, however, going to share with you some insight that I have gained into what some of the common traits of successful online entrepreneurs are. One common thread among these and other successful marketers is the use of AdWords and pay-per-click.

In this chapter, we're talking about writing AdWords and pay-per-click copy. I will talk primarily about AdWords, because it is the

800-pound gorilla in the pay-per-click world, but I want to be clear: I am not an AdWords guru.

I am not going to teach you the inside tricks on how to run AdWords campaigns with Google. I will tell you some of the things that I know that work, but my expertise is marketing, copy, and the technical details of running an AdWords campaign.

There are other people whom I believe are the experts in these areas. They are the people I learned from, so I will point you in their direction. What I'm going to talk about is how to write copy for your AdWords campaign.

I'm going to cover the basics for you as well as provide you with access to free materials from a couple of the top experts on AdWords that you can use to augment the copywriting techniques and tactics that we're going to discuss in this chapter. Combining these items together, you will be able to obliterate your competition when it comes to AdWords. And believe me, AdWords is all about competition.

Here are four steps to get you started.

> **Number one**: Get involved in Google AdWords. Get your own account. This is a powerful conduit for the advertising and promotion of your site, and you will need only a few items. There is a formula for success online. You need to market. You need a group of people who want to buy the item, process, or service that you're selling, and you need to find that market.
>
> **Number two**: You need an offer, something to sell them, a box, a potion, a lotion, an idea, or a service that you provide them. That is your offer.
>
> **Number three:** You need traffic. You need people to actually come, be in front of your offer, read it, and make a decision to buy it. Which means you need something to put in front of them. That something is copywriting and what we're studying in this book. If you have all of those things and you add them together, you get profit. That's the formula.

Number four: You need to study the AdWords campaigns of your competitors. Know what's working, because this is one of the most beautiful forms of advertising I've ever seen.

My background is in the radio industry, where I worked for a couple of decades. I'm familiar with radio, television, newspaper, and direct mail advertising, because we did so much of it in that business.

Most people don't realize that people in the radio industry have to promote their radio stations. How do they do it? Well, have you ever seen a TV ad for a radio station? I bought lots of TV ad space. Have you ever seen a direct mail piece advertising a radio station? I bought lots of direct mail advertising in my days in radio advertising. We also bought newspaper ads and learned about newspaper advertising, because we had to compete against and know our competitors.

Knowing all those different forms of advertising, I was astounded when Google AdWords came along! Here was a form of advertising that you could measure. Not only that, you could turn on the traffic like you were turning on a water spigot. Think about that. You can set up a Google AdWords account, turn on the traffic, and put a thousand visitors in front of your Web page instantly.

You can turn it on just as you would turn on water and test your advertising campaign. If it is not working, you shut the traffic off, make some changes, and then turn it back on. It's an astounding advantage we have that marketers in the past never had. It's exciting! It's an exciting time to be alive and selling things. I believe that this creates opportunities for people to have their own businesses that never existed before in the history of mankind.

People have always been able to sell things. There are marketplaces, and there has been direct marketing for a long time, but never has the barrier to entry been so low. Never have the prospects for success been so likely.

Before we get started with the checklist for this chapter, I'm going to point you to two online resources that I think you should be looking at. One is Perry Marshall, who is the premier AdWords expert. He is the expert that the experts turn to when they want to know about Google AdWords. I think you should be listening to him, too. Go to www.PerryMarshallOnline.com and sign up for his free course, "Five days to success with Google AdWords."

I'm also going to recommend that you take a look at Keyword Elite, which is a powerful piece of software that was created by my client Brad Callen. This software allows you to master the power of Google AdWords.

Mastering these types of ads isn't as easy as it looks. The length of PPC ads belies their power and importance. They're short—only seventy-five or ninety-five characters long in Google AdWords. You might think, "How hard can that be?" I assure you, it is very difficult.

It requires a lot of thought and testing to get the right ninety-five characters—which includes spaces, by the way. You need to give them the focus and level of importance that they deserve.

21 Tips for Better PPC Ads

Let's get right into our list for creating successful, effective AdWords and pay-per-click campaigns.

1) **Target your pay-per-click ads to your buyers.**

   Traffic is a good thing, but targeted traffic that buys your stuff is even better. Why is this important, and why are we even talking about it? The reason is quite simple. It could be easy to write Google AdWords copy that would bring traffic to your site, but it needs to be relevant to what you're offering.

   If it's not relevant and if that traffic isn't targeted, if those people aren't interested in what you're selling, then you're wasting money. Every time someone clicks on a Google AdWords ad, you're paying for that traffic. Don't you want to make sure you're getting the most out of your investment in that traffic?

When you set up your Google AdWords account, you're purchasing the real estate on the right-hand side of the Google page when someone types in a keyword search term. You've done it many times. You've typed in search terms, and over on the right-hand side of the page you have noticed those little boxes. Those are Google ads. When you click on those little boxes, someone somewhere is paying for that click.

So, think about this from a user's perspective: if the ad is misleading, this can give you a bad impression of AdWords. This is why Google can sometimes seem so persnickety in what they will allow you to do in your AdWords campaign. They want the users of Google to have a good experience. That's the only way that Google AdWords advertisers will continue to pay their money. To have a good experience, users need to click on an ad and see relevant material.

You want to target your ad and make sure that it's consistent with what you're offering or what's on your Web page.

2) **Make a compelling statement of benefit in your Google AdWords ad.**

You have ninety-five characters with which to paint the picture of your prospect enjoying the benefits of your offer. If this sounds as though I'm beating a dead horse, it's because I am.

In any ad, whether it is a Google AdWords ad, a radio ad, a sales letter, or a squeeze page, it all has to accomplish one goal: to get an action from your readers.

If you want them to opt-in, to buy, or to click, then the goal you want to accomplish is to paint a picture, in the minds of your prospects or readers, of them enjoying the benefit of your product or service. That's so important! That's why I've mentioned that idea in every single chapter, no matter what we're talking about. You must understand how important that is.

3) **Know the MWR for your ad.**

The MWR, you will recall, is the most wanted response. Know what you want them to do when they read your ad.

Now, the simple answer of course is "Well, I want them to click." OK, I think we all can stipulate that we want them to click, but think about what you want their state of mind to be when they actually do the clicking.

Do you want them to be expecting a free report? If they are, how are you going to deliver that free report? If you just say, "No obligation free report," and bring them to a squeeze page where they have to put in their names and e-mail addresses, then that becomes an obligation. That's not what they expected. They're not going to be happy. You need to think about the way that you're framing your offer and what you want them to do. Think about the best way for you to get the readers or prospects to do what it is you want them to do.

4) **Know your keywords.**

Keywords are the terms people use to find your site or your ad. It's what they type in to Google, or any other search engine for that matter. You need to know what people are typing in if they're searching for your category, product, or service. One mistake that people make is assuming they know instinctively what keywords people are searching under.

It's sometimes very surprising to discover the terms that people put into search engines when they're looking for information, products, or services. For instance, you would be surprised at the number of people who actually type the site's URL into Google. Let's say that they're looking for Flickr.

Flickr is a Web site that allows you to share pictures online and have an online photo album, and many people will go to Google and type in "flickr.com." If you think about that, that doesn't make a whole lot of sense. Why didn't they just type that into the address bar?

My point in telling you this is to simply say, you need to do your homework and find out what people are typing in when they're searching for your product, category, or service. It may not be what you think it is.

Once you figure out what the core keywords are, figure out what the variations are, because sometimes those little side variations will result in a lot of traffic. One variation, for instance, would be a common misspelling of the word people are searching for.

For instance, let's say you're trying to sell a heraldry product on your genealogy Web site. People may know that heraldry refers to family coats of arms, but they may be unsure of the spelling. A common way to get traffic to your heraldry page might be to advertise for "haroldry" or "heraldery" or whatever the most common misspellings are.

Sometimes you'll find that people type in the most surprising keywords when they're looking for your product. It might have nothing to do with what you call your product, because it's all about what your prospects, your readers, call your product—how they refer to it or think about it.

Know your keywords. There are some tools you can use that will help you with this. One of them is a free tool that you can find at GoodKeyWords.com. It will help you do some basic keyword research and find out what people are searching for.

5) **Use your money keywords.**

You must know what your money keywords are and how to use them to generate money. What I mean by this is the fact that the keywords that generate the most traffic are not always the ones that you want to look for.

For instance, "free" is going to be a big keyword in a lot of categories, but people who are searching for free whatever—whether it's free heraldry, free baby clothes, free information—probably aren't interested in spending money, so they may not be your most lucrative customers.

While that's an obvious example, it's not always quite so obvious. You need to be able to do some research and figure out what the most lucrative keywords are and spend your time and your money focusing on getting clicks through those keywords. They are the ones that are going to make you the most money.

6) **Offer an ethical bribe if appropriate.**

If your most wanted result is to generate and capture a lead, you may want to offer an ethical bribe.

For instance, let's say that you're running a Google AdWords campaign and you want to generate leads for a credit card offer. Perhaps you're an affiliate of a credit card company and you get paid—let's say, $50—for every application you bring them; therefore, you want to generate leads for credit card offers.

You might run a pay-per-click campaign. You could send the clicks straight to the offer itself, but of course, if they choose not to take the offer that day, you might never see those people again. You might never see a commission from them.

What if you capture their information, however? What if you have, for instance, a special report that helps people select the right credit card for them? Or perhaps the report helps them get a credit card if they have had trouble getting one in the past. What if, to get this report, they simply give their names and e-mail addresses?

In other words, you're generating leads. You're putting them on your mailing list, so you can continue to make them offers and make more money as a result. You're offering an ethical bribe to get them to give up their contact information. You do, however, need to be careful when offering ethical bribes, which brings up:

7) **Use a bribe barrier to discourage freebie seekers.**

In the example I just gave you, it might be easy for people to give you a fake name and e-mail address or a name and e-mail address they can easily ignore, but if you want to get higher quality leads from your pay-per-click campaigns, you might want to use what I call a bribe barrier.

Sift and sort your traffic for maximum efficiency. This means you want the people who are the buyers, who are the takers of the offer, who are going to make you the most money, right? That's the name of the game.

One way to do that is to just ask for more information. Require it. Require them to give you their address and phone number. That will lower the number of leads you get, but it will improve the quality of those leads. If you do that and you decide to send them offers via postal mail, you will probably want to use a mailing service first, to check the list and make sure the e-mail and postal addresses are real. Get some verification before you spend money sending them direct mail pieces.

8) **Use negative qualifiers to drive down ad costs.**

You can dramatically lower your cost by discouraging clicks. You can use language in your ad itself that will discourage people from clicking on the ad unless they're your true customers.

Negative qualifiers might be language like, "Have you declared bankruptcy?" That's a negative qualifier—you're asking people questions that might eliminate large sections of the viewing public from possibly clicking on your ad.

This is not a bad thing, as it lowers your ad cost by giving you more focused clicks. Focused clicks come from people who are only in the narrow target group that you want to speak to.

9) **Use a call to action.**

Even though it's only ninety-five characters long, this is still an ad we're writing. What's one of the basic parts of an ad? Remember the four-part "brute force" method of selling? The last item was "Tell them what to do." "Here's how to buy, now!" Your call to action is to have them click.

Remember, you can't use that kind of language in your AdWords; you can't say, "Click below," but you can have a call to action that says something like, "Claim your free video, take the self-evaluation test now!" You can use those kinds of calls to action. Remember I said this wasn't easy? It takes some thought, because you only have ninety-five characters to work with.

10) **Promote your USP—your unique selling proposition.**

How do you stand out from your competition? What makes you different? If you find you don't have competition—if you're the only one advertising in your category on Google—you need to explore the possibility of selling something else.

If you're the only one, you may think you're pioneering a new niche that nobody's thought of, one that you're going to make a lot of money in. While that is possible, the odds are against that. I'm not trying to be the bearer of bad news. Hopefully I'm bringing you news that will help save you a lot of wasted money, time, and heartache.

If nobody else is selling your product, it may not be sellable. If you have come up with the idea for a new course that teaches people how to make hats, using a special glass-blowing technique, that people can wear on top of their heads like a tiara, that's a bizarre product, probably not something anybody is going to want to buy.

You might be the only one advertising it on Google, but you may also be the only one reading the ad! That's not a situation you want to be in. So make sure you do have some competition. Keep in mind, though, that competition means that people have other choices. Answering the question of why they would choose you instead is your USP—your unique selling proposition.

In my case, as a copywriter, what would be my unique selling proposition? Well, it could be that Mark Victor Hansen hired me to write his copy, that Jack Canfield hired me to write his copy, or Frank Kern, Alex Mandossian, or any of my other well-known clients.

That's a USP because it implies credibility; it implies people who know what they're doing when it comes to marketing or copywriting are paying me to write their copy. What is your USP? You definitely have one.

There's also something I call the NUSP™—the Niche Unique Selling Proposition. I submit to you that you're better off if you're inside a niche where there is a lot of competition and then find a unique way to differentiate yourself inside that niche.

11) Spy on successful competitors.

Learn what's working for your competitors and use that knowledge against them, to beat them. I promise you this: your competitors aren't doing that. Though they might occasionally look at what everybody else is doing and copy a good idea here or there, they're not being strategic about it.

You can be, if you make a concerted effort. Just put some time on your calendar every week to look at what your competitors are doing on AdWords. You can see what they're doing, what's working for them, and what's not working. How do you know what's not working? Watch what ads they stop running. There's a reason they stopped running them.

You can definitely get inside information on their business. That's one of the interesting things about AdWords; everything is open. Granted, there are certain things you can't see.

For instance, you can't know for sure what your competitors' click-through rates are. You can bet that if they keep showing up near the top of the results it's a successful campaign for them. If you can find out how much it costs to bid on the keywords they're bidding on—which is easy for you to do—then you know a lot.

You know a lot of things you couldn't have known in years gone by, when you were competing against people who were advertising on radio, on television, in newspapers, or with direct mail. With Google and pay-per-click advertising, you can be armed with a lot of your competitors' information.

Most of your competitors won't take the time to learn this information, because it takes work and it takes thought. If you're willing to do a little bit of work, coupled with a little bit of thinking, then you can be far ahead in the game, and you can use their own success against them.

Forgive me if that sounds a bit Machiavellian, but this is a game where we play for keeps, so sometimes you have to take the more aggressive approach.

12) Use Google's tracking tools.

The quality of your traffic is an important thing to measure, and Google has tracking tools built right into its AdWords system.

Google has a split system where you can put in alternate ads and Google will rotate them, find the one that works best, and show that ad more often. Google has analytic software that will show you the paths that people take through your Web sites. You can track the performance of ads inside Google AdWords. If you're using Google AdWords to do your advertising, there is no excuse for not tracking the results from your ads.

There is no excuse for not knowing how to do it. Google has outstanding documentation for its products, which is where you should start. Start by studying the documentation, the how-to's, which have already been created inside your Google accounts, and if you still need more help, just go to Google and type in a search.

Search the phrase "AdWords tutorials." You will find tons of resources online that will help you figure out how to use the tracking tools.

13) Always split test your ads.

Yes, this was part of number twelve, but it bears repeating because it is so easy to do. There's no excuse for not doing it. You should always have a split test of your pay-per-click advertising running—always maximizing your results.

The next five items are specific ad writing tips that will help increase your click-throughs and your profits on your Google AdWords ads.

14) Use your main keyword in the headline.

This is PPC ad writing tip number one. It will increase the number of clicks that you receive. It will increase the number of people who will look at your ad and pay attention to it. I hope that the answer why is obvious.

If I type in "balloons" as my search, because I want to buy balloons, the AdWords that show up on the right-hand side of the page say, "Balloons." Don't you think that is going to get my attention?

You need to use the main keyword in the headline. There is a device you can use inside Google called dynamic keyword insertion. You can write your headline in such a way that the keyword you typed in will show up as part of your headline.

You have seen this in action if you have ever done a search. For instance, let's say you're a music buff and you're looking for Johnny Mathis cassette tapes. You type in "Johnny Mathis." Over on the right-hand side of the page you see an ad that says,

"Johnny Mathis on eBay." That's because eBay made a deal with Google using dynamic keyword insertion, so whatever you type in will show up as a Google ad result for eBay, so you will click on that and go to eBay to buy a Johnny Mathis CD or tape.

Dynamic keyword insertion can work, but I would urge you to be careful about it. Depending on how you use it, you can end up looking silly, because sometimes the results don't make sense. Think about what people might type in and how that might look if it gets inserted into that black spot in your ad before you do it, so that you're not embarrassed later on.

15) Use power words to evoke an emotional response.

This is your PPC ad writing tip number two. You need to be careful when you're using power words. They have a tendency to attract tire kickers and freebie seekers to your site.

Don't use a power word like *free* in your ad, because then you're going to get a bunch of people who are looking for free stuff. If all you want is leads or people to sign up for a newsletter or something, then it might be worth your while to use that word.

Just think about what you want to accomplish and always have your most wanted response in mind when you are putting power words in your ad.

Some power words would include: cheap, sale, special, tricks, tips, discover. Make sure these words serve your greater purpose and that they're consistent with the action that you want your reader to take.

16) Omit needless words.

In our third PPC ad writing tip, I want to remind you that you only have ninety-five characters to make your case. Those ninety-five characters include your headline and the spaces between the words. You need to think carefully about what those ninety-five characters are going to be.

Do not take up valuable real estate by putting words like *the*, *and*, *a*, *of*, and so forth into your ad. Those just eat up space. Find ways to say what you need to say without using those words. Punctuation counts as a character too. Consider carefully if you really need that punctuation before you put it in.

17) Include the price in your ad.

Our fourth PPC ad writing tip is the best way to qualify people. I see this mistake all the time. Let's say you have an e-book that sells for $27.00 as well as a free newsletter about training the dog not to soil the house.

A common mistake would be to phrase your ad, "Get my free newsletter on house-training your dog." Now the newsletter is a leader item to sell them the e-book, but with this ad, what kind of traffic are you going to get? You're going to get people who want your free newsletter but don't want to spend money, which is not a good thing.

A better way to do this would be, "Housebreak your dog in seven days. Guaranteed method, trains your dog like magic, never fails–$27.00." You might think a lot of people aren't going to click on that because they don't want to pay $27.00. You would be right, but remember this is "pay-per-click." If they're not going to spend money, why would you want to pay to have those people click on your ad?

When people click on your page and say, "I'm not going to pay $27.00 for that!" and then go away, it costs you money! You don't want them eating up your advertising budget. This is a good way to get rid of those freebie seekers and tire kickers that cost you money.

On the other hand, if you have a higher priced product, you could be scaring people away by putting the price in your ad. In that case, you may want to offer people something like a piece of software or some other offer to get them to opt-in, so you can continue to market for your expensive product.

You have to think strategically. If you're selling a thousand-dollar product, then you probably don't want to put that price in your Google AdWords ad. I would probably want them to opt-in and receive a special report or something first.

18) Use keyword-focused questions.

In our fifth PPC ad writing tip I want to talk about the importance of asking questions. Questions have been shown to be very powerful in Google AdWords campaigns and other PPC campaigns as well. For instance, let's say your keyword is *copywriting* (an example I'm quite familiar with). You're a copywriter looking for clients, and you run some Google AdWords to get more clients.

They type in the word "copywriting," and they see your ad's headline, which says, "Need copywriting?" That's an attention-grabber, because the answer is, "Yes, I just typed in 'copywriting' and I do need it."

Let's say that a person types in "arthritis relief." He or she is in pain and wants some relief from the pain. Your ad says, "Suffering from arthritis or arthritis pain?" Or let's say a person types in "diet tips," and you have a headline on your ad that says, "Diet tips now" or "Free diet tips" or whatever is appropriate for your offer. Maybe someone types in "weight loss," and your headline says, "Need to lose weight now?"

This is a powerful technique; you'll need to think about it carefully and make sure that it makes sense in your specific case. You also have to play around with the length of your headlines. You only have a very few number of characters.

19) Study the AdWords system.

This deserves more than just your cursory attention. You need to give some thought to how this whole thing works. You need to know how it works before you use it. If you don't, it will cost you a lot of money.

There are many stories of people who thought they knew what they were doing but didn't bother to read the instructions or learn how to use their AdWords account, and before they knew it, they had spent a couple thousand dollars. All that, without even knowing that was what they were about to do. It would have been good if they had spent a little time and learned how the system works. Study it carefully.

20) Don't skimp on tools.

Get good software tools to do your keyword research and manage your pay-per-click campaign. I have a specific tool that I recommend: it's called Keyword Elite. I recommend it because I use it. Go to KeyWordElitePPC.com and watch the videos that demonstrate how the software works. It's really a very good tool.

21) Never take your eye off the ball.

AdWords isn't a "set it and forget it" program. If you set it and forget it, you're going to pay for it. You can get a big shock when you get the e-bill for hundreds or thousands of dollars. This is a valuable lesson. Things change. Click rates change. It's important that you keep on top of it. Watch your results daily.

If you're not watching them daily, then have someone on your team who's watching those results daily, so you know what's going on and don't end up with a lot of expense you didn't expect or anticipate and can't afford.

Here is the real value determiner: what's the value of a click to you? You are going to have to get some traffic to your site to figure this out. If you know that for every thousand people that you get coming to your site, you're going to get a hundred buyers, then you know you're getting a 10 percent conversion rate. If you are selling a product that is $2977.00, then those hundred buyers will net you $29770.00 in sales. Divide that number by those one thousand clicks and that tells you that the value of each click is $29.77. As long as your numbers are reliable, you know you could afford to pay up to $29.00 a click.

Make sure that your data is good. Make sure that you have enough clicks to really know statistically that this works. This is another reason to check your stats daily. If you're in a very competitive market where the clicks cost a lot of money, and you're paying $5 to $12 a click, then you need to make sure you have a good conversion process going so you can convert those leads into buyers.

SUMMARY
AdWords & PPC Copy Explained

1. **Target Your PPC Ads to Buyers.** Traffic may be good, but targeted traffic that buys is best.
2. **Make a Compelling Statement of Benefit.** In just ninety-five characters, you must paint the picture of your prospect enjoying the benefits of your offer.
3. **Know the MWR for Your Ad.** Every mistake will cost you money, so make sure you know what you want.
4. **Know Your Keywords.** Keywords are the terms people use to find your site or your ad. Do you know what they are?
5. **Use Your Money Keywords.** You must know what your money keywords are and how to use them to generate money.
6. **Offer an Ethical Bribe if Appropriate.** If your MWR is to generate and capture a lead, you may want to offer an ethical bribe.
7. **Use a Bribe Barrier to Discourage Freebie Seekers.** Sift and sort your traffic for maximum efficiency.

8. **Use Negative Qualifiers to Drive Down Ad Costs.** Dramatically lower your spending by discouraging clicks.

9. **Use a Call to Action.** This is an ad; tell readers what to do.

10. **Promote Your USP.** How can you stand out? Using the USP and the NUSP.

11. **Spy on Successful Competitors.** Learn what's working for your competitors and use that knowledge.

12. **Use Google's Tracking Tools.** Quality counts.

13. **Always Split Test Your Ads.** It's so easy to do, there's no excuse for not doing it.

14. **PPC Ad Writing Tip #1: Use Your Main Keyword in the Headline.** This will increase the number of clicks you receive.

15. **PPC Ad Writing Tip #2: Use Power Words to Evoke Response.** Words like *cheap, sale, special, tricks, tips, discover* ... but be careful!

16. **PPC Ad Writing Tip #3: Omit Needless Words.** Words that don't help cost money: the, an, a, of, etc.

17. **PPC Ad Writing Tip #4: Include the Price in Your Ad.** Best way to get rid of freebie seekers.

18. **PPC Ad Writing Tip #5: Use Keyword-Focused Questions.** For example... "Need **Copywriting?**"; "Suffering from **Arthritis?**"; "Need to **Lose Weight** Now?"

19. **Study the AdWords System.** You need to know how it works before you use it. Failure to do so can bankrupt you.

20. **Don't Skimp on Tools.** Get good software tools to do your keyword research.

21. **Never Take Your Eye Off the Ball.** AdWords is not a "set it and forget it" program; watch your results daily at a minimum.

Chapter 8

The Secrets of Getting Your Prospects So Excited About You They'll FIGHT for the Privilege of Buying Your Stuff

"Oh yeah, one more thing..."

—Steve Jobs

...on "launch day" every year, just before he unveils the one thing everyone really wants to hear about (OSX, iPod, iPod video, iPhone, etc.)

The quote starting off this chapter is one of my favorite examples of a product launch. It's from Steve Jobs of Apple Computer. He always says, "One more thing..." like the old detective on TV, Columbo. On launch day every year at the big Apple announcement, Steve Jobs makes his keynote presentation about the company, then he announces the exciting new product last.

It may be OSX, or it might be the iPod, iPod video, or the iPhone, as it was this year, but he's become famous for uttering those words every year just before he unveils the one thing everybody really came to hear about.

He knows nobody came to hear about the health of the company, the future of the industry, and all that stuff. They came to hear about the brand-new ultra-cool product that Apple's about to launch. Steve has made it a tradition of pretending to end his presentation and finally saying, "Oh yeah, one more thing…" It's what people were waiting for. When you see that happen, that is a product launch in action.

It follows all of the principles of a product launch. For those of you who are not familiar with this phenomenon yet, a "product launch" within the online marketing world refers to a very specific set of actions, behaviors, and marketing and promotion tactics.

This includes the sending of lots of e-mails from joint venture partners about one particular program, product, or offering and usually the release of a big special report or PDF and then a launch day with a limited number of units, memberships, boxes, or whatever available. These are all tactics of the product launch formula.

This was something originated, codified, and taught by Jeff Walker, who is a client and friend of mine. I've been involved in his coaching program, and he was instrumental in helping to launch my Web Copywriting Explained course.

I want to give you a little background about the origins of the product launch methodology. Jeff has been the go-to guy behind the scenes for all of the biggest product launches in the online marketing world. He engineered John Reese's million-dollar day for the launch of Traffic Secrets.

Jeff was involved in every major launch over the course of the last eighteen months online in some way, shape, form, or fashion. He's been involved in product launches that have a total value of over $31 million.

He's certainly somebody who knows about the product launch process, and many, if not all, of the things I've learned about product launches, I learned from Jeff. Much of the material in this chapter grew out of conversations that Jeff and I had about product launches and how they relate to copy.

When you have a sale, or a promotion for your product, you make a special effort to sell it, and you do so by telling stories about it. Those three particular activities—launches, promotions, and story selling—are inextricably intertwined in my mind. I don't think you can separate the three.

Any time you do a promotion, you're doing a miniature launch. Any time you're doing story selling, you are in a way launching or re-launching that product, and certainly, any time you do a product launch, you are doing a promotion and you are using story selling, if you're doing the product launch correctly.

The first thing you need to do is decide what kind of launch you're going to do. Are you going to do a full launch, one that's going to last over a period of several weeks from beginning to end? Are you going to do a compressed launch, which might be a process of launching your product over the period of a week to ten days, or are you going to do a mini-launch, which could be more like a promotion that takes place over one to three days?

When we talk about the time frame these launches need, it's important to keep in mind that a product launch consists of a sequence of marketing events that form a story. There's something very powerful at work here, and that is the Zeigarnik effect. Remember, that's the effect discovered by Bluma Zeigarnik, who noted people tend to remember things that are incomplete.

The incomplete loop in your mind draws and magnetizes your attention, so when you have a sequence of marketing events—for instance, a sequence of e-mails, pieces of sales copy, blog posts, PDF reports, videos, and audios—there is a need in the human psyche to complete the sequence, to finish the story.

Your next step is to map out your own launch. Plan it on a calendar, even if you're doing a promotion, not a launch. Think of it like a launch and at the very least, map out the beginning, middle, and end on the calendar. That will give you a framework to plan your launch and make it more effective.

Number three is going to include the most blatant recommendation of a product I'm going to make in this entire book. Study Jeff Walker's material, *The Product Launch Formula*. If you don't already own a copy, you need to get a copy of this course. Later in this chapter, we'll look at Jeff's own product launch strategy and how he's done an on-going launch of his products. You can study his material for yourself at www.TheProductLaunchFormula.com.

We're also going to look at Rich Schefren's launch for StrategicProfits.com, which was a massively successful launch where he did over $3.5 million in one week. We're going to look at some of the launch tactics employed by my own launch and for a couple client projects I did for Matt Bacak, including *The Internet Marketing Dirt* and *Internet Millionaire Mind*.

If you're marketing on the Internet, you're always doing a product launch. The only question is, are you doing it well or doing it poorly? Your copy, your Web site, is telling a story. Whether you're consciously directing that story and deciding what you want the effects of that story to be, is up to you.

If you let it happen unconsciously, you may not be happy with the results. If you consciously direct that story and think about the strategy behind it, and make the tactics fit the strategy, then you can improve your results in almost every case.

21 Tips for Better Product Launches

Here's twenty-one points to remember regarding product launches, promotions, and story selling:

1) **Product launch copy sets the frame.**
   Product launches work because they employ all the factors of the psychology of influence. This subject was examined in detail by Dr. Robert Cialdini in his book, *Influence*.

   That book is the result of university peer-reviewed studies demonstrating the factors that influence people's behavior. One of those factors is the law of reciprocity. If I give you a gift, you feel a debt of gratitude. You feel you need to return that gift. That is the power of reciprocity.

Another psychological factor is social proof. We look to see what other people are doing to verify whether or not our behavior is correct. There's the principle of liking. There's the principle of scarcity. We tend to want things if we know they are scarce and not many people have them.

Jeff Walker took the factors spelled out in that book by Dr. Cialdini and integrated them into a sequential marketing system called "The Product Launch Formula." That's the reason why that formula is so powerful, because it employs all those factors that are outlined in that book in a very systematic fashion that influences behavior in a very predictable way.

One of the things Jeff Walker has been famous for saying is that his goal in setting up a product launch is to make the sales letter irrelevant. I think that's a bit of an overstatement. I don't think the sales letter is irrelevant. I think it becomes less crucial if the product launch is done correctly, but the fact is, the entire launch is copy. There's a lot of copy that's involved in doing a product launch, which leads us to…

2) **Launch copy begins long before the sales letter.**
In fact, the sales letter, even though it might be sizable (some recent launches have had one-hundred-page sale letters!), may only represent 10–20 percent of the actual copy used in the product launch.

A product launch will typically involve copy that begins when a simple list-building site is put up. It could be blog posts, then e-mails, surveys, survey questions, and articles. Copy that's written to recruit partners. Copy that your partners can send out to their lists to help launch your product. There is an entire sequence of e-mails, both before and after the launch.

There's the actual sales letter itself. There's follow-up e-mail. That's a lot of copy involved!

The sales letter only represents a portion of the copy that gets written for a product launch. It's not irrelevant, because all the psychological factors, when coupled with the other copy, put the potential buyers into a certain frame of mind so that when they come to the sales letter, they're more likely to be influenced to buy. In fact, they may have already made their decision to buy and are just looking for a "Buy Now" button to push.

3) **Product launches are first a story.**

The most effective way to set the launch up for success is to do so by making it into a story. The story might be as simple as, "I had a problem, and I figured out a way to solve it. Now, I would like to share with you how I solved that problem."

That could be the beginning of a product launch story. If you do nothing but write a bunch of blatant hard-hammering sales messages, you're not going to have much of a launch, because people need a story to engage them emotionally.

4) **Know the arc of your story.**

Space limits forbid me from speaking on the whole art and science of storytelling, but there are some fantastic books about the subject that I will submit to you. I believe the best books on storytelling are not necessarily written by marketers or copywriters. I believe the best books on storytelling are written by storytellers.

There's a book called *Story*, by Robert McKee, which I recommend you get and study. It has a lot to say about telling dynamic, powerful stories. It's mostly read by those who write screenplays, but there is a lot for you to learn from this book. Also, the book *On Writing* by Stephen King is an outstanding resource that will tell you much about storytelling.

For the purposes of our discussion, remember that your product launch is a story and there must be an arc to your story at its simplest level.

A story has a beginning, a middle, and an end. Your launch needs to have the same thing: a feeling of resolution at the end. In that moment of resolution at the end of your launch, you also want to leave people wanting more.

5) **Storyboard your launch on a calendar.**

You want to keep yourself on track during the process of your launch by having a plan that's disciplined by dates. Some of you might be thinking: "Ray, I'm not real sure what the elements of my story need to be, so how will I know how to put that on a calendar?"

Let me walk you through a thumbnail sketch scenario of what your launch might be like. Let's say you're launching a product that's about how to house-train your dog. You've figured out a miracle method for house-training a dog that only takes two or three days.

This is something a lot of pet owners would love to know about. They want to hear your story. They want to hear how you discovered this method. They want to hear how you bought your new pet and how that pet had house-training problems and how you were desperately searching for a solution.

Your launch process could start with something as simple as putting up a blog or perhaps going to forums where pet owners hang out and putting up a post that says, "I'm working on putting together a report on how to house-train your dog; do you guys have any questions about that?"

Take some of those answers and begin to form the basis of your launch. Maybe you blog about some of the struggles that you had with training your dog. Then a few days later, you begin posting about how you've discovered a method that seems to be working.

Just make sure it's all true. Your stories should always be true. I hope that goes without saying. Do not tell lies. You're better than that and don't need to do that. You can always find a real story.

If you didn't have the experience of discovering the method that allowed you to teach your dog to not soil the carpet in three days, but instead you acquired the rights to a product that teaches people how to do that, what's the story there? How about this: "I have a dog that kept having accidents in the house, so I found this product that taught me how to fix the problem and it did, so I bought the rights to the product."

That's a darn good story. In fact, you've heard that story in a famous marketing campaign. It wasn't about dog training; it was about electric shavers. Remember Victor Kiam and the Remington company? "I liked this razor so much, I bought the company."

Map out on a calendar when you're going to release these pieces of the story. Then set a date and tell the people on your mailing list, who read your blog or who read in those forums you frequented, that on May 23rd you're going to open the doors and have fifty copies to sell of this book you've had printed up with the DVD. If they want one, they need to get on the waiting list and be ready to go.

Then you're going to update people, perhaps by sending them an e-mail to let them know, "Now we have one hundred people on the waiting list, so it's important when we open the doors on the 23rd that you move quickly and buy your copy." Once it's sold out, you send them another message, make another blog post, and make up your sales letter describing the product.

You can begin to see how these represent points on a calendar. Laying these points out on the calendar is what I mean by "storyboarding" your launch.

6) **Cast your story.**

Who are the players? I want you to think about this carefully, because you need to think through who the viewers of your story might be, who the potential customers or prospects are, and who the players in your story are.

For instance, if you want your joint venture partners to send an e-mail to their list telling their subscribers about your product or service, you're going to need to write copy that persuades them to do that.

It's the same for affiliates. You'll need a story for your present subscribers, your list members, and a story for new customers, prospects, partners, and the marketing community in general. Remember, they're observing the process of your launch to see how well it goes—to observe your skill as a marketer.

The next eleven points will get into the actual copy components of a launch.

7) **List-building copy.**

(Launch copy component number one.) This is where you're writing copy that starts building a list, perhaps using a blog or commenting in a forum.

One way to do this is, setting up a squeeze page somewhere, then making posts to your blog that talk about the fact that you're conducting a survey for a book you're thinking about writing or for some articles you want to create.

If it's in a community where a lot of activity and communication takes place naturally, then it could just be as simple as saying, "I'm taking a survey of iguana owners. What are the biggest problems you face as an iguana owner? What are the best things about owning an iguana? What are your funniest iguana stories?" I know I'm picking a ridiculous market as an illustration, but this idea will work in any market.

Then you need copy for your squeeze page. You need copy for your confirmation e-mail. You need copy for your follow-up e-mail, and you're going to need to think about how that continues to tell your story.

8) **Your survey**.

(Launch copy component number two.) As your list and traffic grow, you want to start asking your market what bugs them. Find out what their pain is.

There are two ways to go about this when you're thinking about how you're going to create and market your product. You can focus on relieving a certain pain in the life of the prospect or you can focus on moving the prospect towards some type of pleasurable outcome.

People will respond more readily and will do more to get out of pain than to get into pleasure. I tend to want to focus on the pain-relieving aspects of the product or service.

You could just as easily focus on the pleasure-inducing aspect. That would be good in hobby markets, for instance, such as the model train market. People do model train activities because those activities make them feel good, not because they relieve some great deep psychological pain. That's a choice you are going to want to make. I recommend focusing on finding their pain and ways to relieve it.

9) **Product**.

(Launch copy component number three.) This is especially important if you're creating an information product. You want to think of your product itself as copy because it's making a continual sale to your buyer. The sale it's making is, "I was worth investing in. I am giving you value."

You need to think in terms of how you structure the product, how it is written in language that reaffirms the decision the prospect made when he or she decided to invest in it. Make sure it addresses the questions and points that were in the copy that sold it to begin with. How many times have you purchased an information product and after you bought it, read it, listened to it, or watched the videos wondered, "What happened to those bullet points that made me buy this? I don't even see where those are answered."

You want to make sure you address those in the product itself. Think of the product as an extension of your copy.

10) JV recruitment copy.

(Launch copy component number four.) This is joint venture recruitment copy. When you're performing a launch, you don't want to rely on just your own list. What if you don't have a list; you're starting from scratch, and you need to create a list from nothing?

The way you do that is with joint venture partners. Let's say, for instance, you are a veterinary doctor and you created a product on treating your pet for common ailments at home: "How to do preventative health care with your pet at home and how to use holistic remedies for your pet, natural remedies at home to save the expense and have a healthier pet."

Let's say you created this product, and you have good information, but you have no list. This very situation was faced by my coaching and copywriting client Dr. Andrew Jones. He created the product I just spoke of and did over $44,000 in his first week, creating an on-going income stream based on this product with no e-mail list.

How did he do this? He got joint venture partners. He called other vendors who offered products to the market he wanted to speak to: pet owners who care about their pets. He said to them, "I'm going to have this product. If you will send an e-mail to the folks on your e-mail list, and they buy from your e-mail, then I will give you half of the proceeds from that sale."

This was an idea many people he spoke with had never heard of before. Outside of the Internet marketing world, this is news to people. It's so exciting to take these techniques and put them to work outside the "marketing" market, where people are teaching other people how to make money by selling stuff to people who want to teach people how to make money. That's JV recruitment!

11) Pre-launch copy.

(Launch copy component number five.) The next few components are all part of this. Here is where you begin building anticipation, scarcity, and social proof. Get your market as excited about your launch as you are.

12) The big PDF.

(Launch copy component number six.) This is where you're going to write a white paper, a position paper or special report that spells out your platform or USP (unique selling proposition). It needs to really grab people's attention.

Mike Filsaime did this recently with something called "The Death of Internet Marketing." My colleague Michel Fortin did it with something called "Death of the Sales Letter." (Don't worry, the sales letter isn't dead.) Of course, John Reese did it with his Traffic Secrets launch. You'll notice one of the qualities of all these million-dollar launches is that they each employ some form of the big PDF. Rich Schefren had three big PDFs in his launch process. As I said earlier, he did over $3 million in a single week.

13) Unpredictable plot complications.

(Launch copy component number seven.) We're borrowing language from television and movie script writers now. "Unpredictable plot complications" means things will occur you didn't plan for. Some people identify them as problems; I like to identify them as storytelling opportunities.

Let's say your server goes down. That's the one that people know most commonly. "Our server went down; we had so much traffic from people who wanted to get a copy of our big PDF that our server went down."

That's a story, but it's a story that's been told so often inside the Internet marketing market, it might have lost some of its effectiveness. You might want to look for a different story to tell.

Maybe you got a nasty e-mail from someone who doesn't like the way you're promoting your product or offer. Share that with the people on your pre-launch list and let them see the story unfold. I promise you, if you do that, you'll win the hearts of the people on your list. Your prospects will leap to your defense. (I know because it happened to me during my own launch.)

Maybe you've got a story of how you had an important meeting that was related to setting up your product, service, or new business, and you locked your keys in the car and couldn't get to your meeting on time, and you felt like the whole thing might crumble. Luckily, you were able to get inside your car and you made it to the meeting.

That's a story. Again, make certain your stories are true—be open to them, and I promise you they will occur. A product launch is such a complex endeavor, things will happen. Things will go wrong; unexpected things will occur. It's not always a problem; sometimes it's a great opportunity.

You might get an unexpected phone call from Tony Robbins' office and he says to you, "I need you to come speak at the Learning Annex; we're having a big event, and I've heard about your products. I would love to have you on the stage at the same time as me, so you can speak about whatever it is you teach."

Wouldn't that be a story worth telling? Yes, it's exaggerated. Yes, it's dramatic. But it actually did happen to one of my clients!

Those kinds of stories make for great storytelling opportunities during your product launch.

14) Countdown copy.

(Launch copy component number eight.) This is where we start playing on the anticipation and scarcity. Again, this is taking a leaf from the book by Robert Cialdini. We're letting people know, "On this date, you will be able to buy tickets to this workshop. You'll be able to buy one of the kits for our product that teaches you how to have a better relationship, but we've only had 100 printed! You will need to be ready when the countdown reaches zero on date (x) at time (x)."

Countdown copy is very effective. Yes, you've seen it done in the marketing world. I know it still works in Internet marketing, and it works even better in markets outside the marketing world, so make sure you include countdown copy as one of your copy components in your launch.

15) The sales letter.

(Launch copy component number nine.) You knew we had to get to this sooner or later! A carefully crafted sales letter is key to the success of your launch. There have been a couple stupendously successful online product launches over the last year. In a couple of cases, a controversy arose over the sales letter.

On one side of the controversy, some people said, "Wow, Copywriter X must be great. He wrote a letter for that product launch and brought in a million dollars in a single day!" (In one case, a million dollars in less than an hour!)

On the other side of the controversy, people were saying, "The sales letter was irrelevant! You could have just put a 'Buy Now' button on that page and people would have bought. You didn't need a sales letter; it had nothing to do with it."

What's the truth? Are sales letters irrelevant in the face of product launches? I don't believe so, and I'm in good company. Michel Fortin doesn't believe they're irrelevant. Jeff Walker, creator of Product Launch Formula, doesn't either, even though he's gone on record as saying his job is to try to make them irrelevant.

I believe what Jeff was saying is that by setting the context with all the other copy components and marketing pieces and activities that take place around a launch, some people will decide to buy before the sales letter even shows up.

Rich Schefren has gone on record as saying many of the people who bought into his coaching program said they made the decision before they ever saw the sales letter. It's because of all the other marketing that he did, like those three big PDFs he released before he released the sales letter.

Those PDFs were actually sales copy. That was all marketing that led to many people deciding to buy before they saw the final sales letter. But there was also a certain number of people who had to see the sales letter before they made the purchasing decision. For those people especially, the sales letter is not irrelevant. In fact, I contend it is key to the success of your launch.

16) Post-launch-week copy.

(Launch copy component number ten.) As much as 30 percent of your sales may come in the week after your big launch day. Think about that. If you don't do any post-launch e-mails, blog posts, or marketing activities, if you don't have any post-launch e-mails for your joint venture partners or affiliates to send out, then you're leaving loads of money on the table. You need to make sure those e-mails are carefully crafted, planned, and ready to go.

17) The missing piece.

(Launch copy component number eleven.) I see this component left out all the time: following up with your buyers and prospects to make your launch become a profitable business.

Often during the process of a launch, a marketer builds a list of potential buyers, then stops marketing after the big launch day, or at least after launch week.

If you're in the small percentage of marketers who are savvy enough to continue marketing the week after the launch, the "missing piece" is to continue to follow up with the people on that list, because they were interested in what you had to offer. They were interested in what you had to say.

Continue talking with them, dialoguing with them, and making offers to them. Just because they didn't buy your initial launch offer, it doesn't mean they may not be interested in other things.

18) Promotions are mini-launches.

If you take the entire process and all the copy components I just outlined and compressed those into a couple of days, you have a promotion, or a mini-launch.

The best promotions are a story. Even a sale, like a back-to-school sale, is a story. The story is, "Summer's over; the kids need some new clothes for school; they need some school supplies. We're going to put those things on sale to help you out because we know you need the help, so come to our Back-to-School Sale. It's good for a few days only." There's your scarcity, urgency, and timeline on the calendar. It's a mini-launch.

19) The magic power of "story selling".

Stories are the process by which we learn, live, and believe anything. I'd like you to think about that carefully and test that statement. Don't just nod your head and say, "Yes, that's good information, Ray." Think it through.

Try to think of something you've learned and lived through, something that you believe, that is not expressed as a story. I don't think you can. I think there's a story even in how you learn to add and subtract. There's a story about those marks on the paper.

20) It takes a village to launch a product.

Product launches are a team sport. There is a false perception that you can sit in your basement at home, dream up a product, type it out, create it on your computer, get online and find your JV partners, launch it, and do it all by yourself.

First of all, if you have JV partners or affiliates, you're not doing it by yourself. Secondly, the most successful product launches involve a number of minds working actively together sculpting and crafting the story as the launch progresses. If you keep this in mind and involve other people in what you're doing, you'll find your launch to be much more successful, because it really is a team sport.

We don't live independent of one another, as we so often think. In Internet marketing, especially, we're inter-dependent. The more you keep that principle in mind, the more successful your launch will be.

21) The one must-own resource.

I've already mentioned this before, but I wanted to emphasize how important this is to get the maximum impact from your launch. You need to own, study, and follow the Product Launch Formula. Again, that link is www.TheProductLaunchFormula.com.

I don't have a very long list of must-own products. I have a long list of really helpful information products, DVDs, books, e-books, and services that help me in my business and that I've seen help my clients and colleagues, but the list of products I would say you *must* have is short, and Product Launch Formula is on that list.

I don't know how to give a stronger endorsement than that. I was one of the first customers of Product Launch Formula. I bought it the day it was released, and it's been a resource that I've used continuously ever since.

SUMMARY
Launch Copy, Promotions, and Story Selling Explained

1. **Product Launch Copy Sets the Frame.** The reason why product launches work is they employ all factors of the psychology of influence.

2. **Launch Copy Begins Long Before the Sales Letter.** The sales letter may be only 10–20 percent of the actual copy for the launch.

3. **Product Launches Are First … a Story.** The most effective way to set the context for a launch is through a story.

4. **Know the "Arc" of Your Story.** A story has a beginning, a middle, and an end. And … a sequel.

5. **Storyboard Your Launch on a Calendar.** Keep yourself on track by having a plan that is disciplined by dates.

6. **Cast Your Story: Who Are the Players?** Think through who the "viewers" of your story might be and who the players are (joint venture partners, affiliates, list members, customers, partners, and … the marketing community).

7. **Launch Copy Component #1: List Building.** Write copy that starts building a list using a blog.

8. **Launch Copy Component #2: Survey.** As your list and traffic grow, start asking your market what bugs them; find their pain.

9. **Launch Copy Component #3: Product.** Think of your product as copy.

10. **Launch Copy Component #4: JV Recruitment.** Your first sale is to your joint venture partners.

11. **Launch Copy Component #5: Pre-Launch Copy.** Begin building the feelings of anticipation, scarcity, and social proof.

12. **Launch Copy Component #6: The "Big PDF."** Write a white paper or special report that spells out your platform or USP.

13. **Launch Copy Component #7: Unpredictable Plot Complications.** Be ready to tell the story you didn't anticipate.

14. **Launch Copy Component #8: Countdown Copy.** Use copy to whip your buyers into a buying frenzy.

15. **Launch Copy Component #9: Sales Letter.** A carefully crafted sales letter is key to the success of your launch.

16. **Launch Copy Component #10: Post-Launch Week.** As much as 30 percent of your sales may come in the week after launch day.

17. **Launch Copy Component #11: The Missing Piece.** Follow up with your buyers and prospects to make your launch into a business.

18. **Promotions Are Mini-Launches.** Compress the process and have a "mini- launch."

19. **The Magic Power of Story Selling.** Stories are the process by which we learn, live, and believe ... anything.

20. **It Takes a Village to Launch a Product.** Product launches are a team sport.

21. **The One MUST-OWN Resource.** To get the maximum impact from your launch, you need to own, study, and follow the Product Launch Formula: www.TheProductLaunchFormula.com.

Chapter 9

Putting It All Together: Secrets of Writing Blockbuster Copy (by Watching Movies)

In the course of writing some blockbuster promotions (a number of my sales letters have brought in seven-figure paydays for my clients), I've seen what works when it comes to copy.

I've also written some promotions that did not work so well on the first run. It pains me to admit that—and these cases are few and far between—but that's the unvarnished truth.

Comparing the many successful pieces of copy I've written, I've identified what I believe is the single biggest difference between copy that rocks (i.e., converts like crazy) and copy that sucks.

I believe that you can inject this one element into any anemic, pathetic, lackluster piece of copy…and transform that underperforming sales letter into an order-getting engine of prosperity.

How did I stumble upon this "secret"?

Watching movies.

More specifically, watching movie *trailers.*

Putting It All Together:

What Makes a Blockbuster Movie Trailer

Of course, you and I know that not all the movies live up to the trailer. We've all had that experience of seeing the actual film and saying, "Well, they put all the *best* parts in the previews."

So, just for the moment, let's think of your product as the movie. And let's think of your sales copy as the "trailer." And just for now, let's assume your product or offer lives up to the promise of the trailer.

So, nobody's going to see the movie—or buy your product—and then want their money back. Nobody's going to say, "The best parts were in the previews."

Can we agree to that, oh Constant Marketer?

Okay. Then the question becomes ... how do we create a "trailer"— in our case, a sales letter—that makes people decide on the spot that they must have the actual product?

The secret of great movie trailers—and of great sales copy—is something I call the dominant story idea, or "DSI" for short.

How the DSI Transforms Copy from Boring to Blockbuster

I'm going to give you an example of how this whole DSI thing can actually save your bacon and turn a losing sales letter into a winner (in just a few minutes).

The best and most successful movie trailers do three things without fail:

1. Give you the dominant story idea (DSI)
2. Offer a sample of the feelings you'll get from the movie itself
3. Provide proof that the movie "works"

Want proof? No problem.

I've selected a couple of example movie trailers, and we'll assume you saw the trailer or a TV commercial for the movies we're discussing. If you really want to see them for yourself, a brief visit to YouTube will get you the trailers in question.

Our first example is for the movie *21*, starring Kevin Spacey.

1. **Dominant story idea:** College math whiz uses his skills to beat the Vegas casinos, gets seduced by the dark side, and gets into trouble with some very bad guys.

2. **Sample feelings:** We see Ben Campbell in his innocent phase…we see him winning…we see him getting seduced by money, power, and very hot women…and then we see him getting into some really scary trouble. Will he prevail?

3. **Proof the movie "works":** We're shown Kevin Spacey, Kate Bosworth, and Laurence Fishburne (proven actors we love)… some very compelling scenes (tightly edited)…and in the background we're anchored by the sound of the Doors singing "Break on Through to the Other Side."

Our second example is, incidentally, just about the same story— but this movie comes from a few years back (1993). It's *The Firm*, based on John Grisham's book. I chose it to make a point: you don't have to come up with a new idea to have a hit. You just need to tell the story in a fresh way.

Here's a summary of *The Firm*, starring Tom Cruise.

1. **Dominant story idea:** Young lawyer passes the bar and gets a dream job—with great pay and even a free BMW. Seems too good to be true. In fact, it is: he's working for the Mob. And if he wants out, they're going to kill him.

2. **Sample feelings:** We see Mitch McDeer in his innocent phase…we see him winning the new job, the car, and the status he so desperately wants…we see him getting seduced by money, power, and very hot women…and then we see him getting into some really scary trouble. Will he prevail? (Hmm. Sounds familiar.)

3. **Proof the movie "works":** Overtly, we're shown Tom Cruise, Gene Hackman, and Hal Holbrook (proven actors we love)… some very compelling scenes (tightly edited) … and in the

background we're anchored by the sound of suspenseful and ominous music (hinting that bad things are about to happen to dear Mitch McDeer).

Back to my point: how this applies to your copy.

Using the DSI to Create Winning Sales Copy

Well, it should be getting clear for you by now…you need to do these same three things with your copy.

As long as your product actually solves a problem, this formula will work for you. All you need to do is figure out how to do the following:

1. **Showcase your dominant story idea:** Imagine you're making a Hollywood movie trailer…how would you sum up your DSI? Look at the movie examples above for some clues.

2. **Offer sample feelings:** Again, looking to our movie trailer examples, can you show—in your copy—some scenes that will help the readers feel the feelings they want to get from your product? You do this by telling stories and directing the readers' imaginations so that they see themselves in the end state your product provides (financial freedom, quitting their job, being a best-selling author, enjoying their new car, or whatever your product does for them). And here's a key: they must link this end state to your product. Let me be clear: by the time they're done with your copy, they need to see that the only way they can reasonably expect to get to that end state is…using your product.

3. **Provide proof the product "works":** You do this in the ways we're familiar with: testimonials, case studies, before-and-after photos and videos, screenshots, etc. Showing "celebrity" endorsements will improve your results by multitudes. Just remember you don't need Kevin Spacey or Tom Cruise… chances are your niche has its own celebrities that will work just as well (or even better) for your purposes.

So how does this work in actual practice?

Let's look at a couple of recent well-known examples and see if we can detect the presence of the DSI.

Frank Kern's "Mass Control" info-product product launch:

1. **Dominant story idea:** Good ol' lovable surfer from California discovers magical techniques that cause mass numbers of people to do whatever he says. These techniques have made Frank millions of dollars and made his buddies tens of millions. And it turns out it's so simple, anybody could do it.

2. **Sample feelings:** Frank tells a story during his launch—not just in the sales letter—that lets the reader imagine himself or herself in the hero's role. We can see ourselves being surprised that this stuff works so well. We're amazed that it works for other people too. We suddenly find ourselves living the dream life…moving to the beach, growing out our hair, and learning to surf. Best of all, we're hanging out with millionaire buddies we've always idolized. And now, we're happy to share our good fortune with others.

3. **Proof the product "works":** Frank actually gave away sample pieces of his product during the launch, and then "everyday people" reported back on their results before the product went on sale. How's that for proof? But Frank didn't stop there—he provided real examples of work he did for his celebrity buddies, and he had a ton of testimonials and case studies to back up all his claims.

Armand Morin's "Internet Marketing Explained" info-product launch:

1. **Dominant story idea:** Making money on the Internet is not as hard as people make it out to be, and Armand (who makes over $20 million per year working from home) can show you every simple step.

2. **Sample feelings:** Armand actually used an interesting tactic for providing sample feelings...he made a whole series of instructional videos and gave them away during his launch. He listened to the feedback from his viewers and let that dictate the content of upcoming videos. By the time he was done, all his prospects had actually experienced the feeling of learning valuable techniques from Armand—and many had made money by using those techniques.

3. **Proof the product "works":** First, Armand let people experience the results themselves. Then, in his sales copy, he provided the credible testimonials and other proof elements we're all familiar with. Finally, he did a marathon teleseminar, which was basically one "celebrity guest" after another telling the story of how using the information in IME had made them a lot of money.

Putting the DSI to Work in Your Own Copy … Today

You might be tempted to say, "That's great for Internet marketing gurus, Ray, but how does it work for me? I just want to juice up my sales letter and get some sales of my product...which has nothing to do with Internet marketing!"

No problem.

Let me give you an action plan for using the DSI method in your marketing. And you can start immediately—as in, today.

First, you need to identify the three elements used by movie studios to "sell" their movies to the public. So, thinking in terms of your own product:

1. What's the dominant story idea of your sales copy? *(For example, "Weird exercise routine provides world's best workout in just 4 minutes" or "Collapsing financial markets have produced an overlooked opportunity for investors," etc.)*

2. What are three ways you can provide sample feelings for your readers ... so they picture themselves using your product and enjoying its benefits? *(For example, can you tell them a true but amazing story? Show them a brief video? Let them try one of your techniques?)*

3. What are three powerful ways you can prove your product works? *(For example, celebrity endorsements, before-and-afters, well-known examples, etc.)*

Once you've actually written these things down, your next task is to incorporate them into your copy. How do you do that? Simple.

Get the DSI into your headline and lead.

This might mean you have to ditch that worn-out "Who Else" headline ... but are you really going to cry about that? For instance, in one of the examples above, I could actually just use my DSI as the headline:

World's Best Workout ... In Just 4 Minutes

Next, summarize your sample feelings elements and place them in the deck copy (right under the headline). Bullet points work best here. To continue using our exercise example, I might write:

In this special report, you will learn the amazing (but true) story behind the world's fastest workout. You'll discover:

❑ **How this method of "fast exercise" was discovered, and how scientific testing has proven it to be effective.**

❑ **The "miracle transformation" that took the method's inventor from 300 points to 160... lowered his blood pressure... and took 30 years off his biological age (and how you can do the same – or better).**

❑ **The principles behind the 4-minute workout and how you can start using them right now to build your strength and endurance.**

But ... How Do I *Find* My DSI?

I've actually left the most important question until the end.

If you've looked at your product and decided that you just don't know what makes it different from any other, don't despair. I can show you *why* you need not despair with a simple exercise: can you name the following movie?

Young man discovers he is destined for greater things, is taken under the wing of a wise older man, and must undertake a great quest to fulfill his destiny. He passes through many grueling trials, but in the end triumphs over the forces of evil and wins the day.

Hmmm.

Star Wars?

The Lord of the Rings?

Batman Begins?

Superman?

Karate Kid?

The answer is ... any or all of the above. And hundreds of other movies as well. While they are each, in essence, the same story, they are also each unique. They all have a very different DSI.

So how do you find your *own* unique DSI?

This is the part I can't put into a formula for you—you've got to do the work yourself. But here are some tips that will help you ...

- ❑ Immerse yourself in your own product. Know it inside and out.
- ❑ Read copy from other markets (different products entirely) and ask, "How MIGHT this story apply to my own product?"
- ❑ Watch the news. What are the top stories and how could they be tied to your promotion?
- ❑ Ask yourself this question: if your product were a movie, what movie would it be? And then see if you can "theme" your product around that idea. Roy Williams, a radio advertising expert, thought of himself as something like the "Wizard of

Oz" … and in a flash of insight branded himself as "The Wizard of Ads." Can you do something similar with your product or service?

What To Do Now

If you can find your own dominant story idea and build your sales copy around it, you'll almost certainly increase your sales and profits. I can promise you, your competition is almost certainly not doing any of this.

Look, it's not just me saying it.

David Ogilvy, arguably one of the greatest ad writers who ever lived, said this:

"Unless your advertising contains a Big Idea, it will pass like a ship in the night. I doubt if more than one campaign in a hundred contains a Big Idea."

Now you know what will set your campaign (or sales letter or product launch) apart from all the others: it's your DSI.

Spend some time identifying it and incorporating it into your copy.

The results will be your reward!

About The Author

Ray Edwards is a sought-after Direct Response Copywriter, Internet Marketing Strategist and internationally-known conference speaker. His clients include New York Times Best-selling authors Jack Canfield and Mark Victor Hansen (creators of Chicken Soup for the Soul), Joel Comm (author of Twitter Power and the Adsense Code), Raymond Aaron (author of Double Your Income Doing What You Love) as well as Armand Morin, Alex Mandossian, Jeff Walker, and many others.

FREE Membership

Claim Your FREE Membership And Bonuses ... A $197 Value for Book Buyers Only!

Good Copy Is A Marketing Multiplier And One Of The Most Reliable Money-Making Skills There Is!

With good copy, almost immediately, you can...

- **Create a steady stream of interested leads and prospects** (instead of being a "nobody" online)...
- **Get more prospects to turn into paying customers** (instead of just "professional browsers")...
- **Stuff your bank account with consistent amounts of fresh cash** (instead of watching the numbers dwindle down each month)...
- **Crush your competition** (instead of letting them take the lion's share of the market)...

And take almost ANY website—in ANY market—from zero to amazing levels of success in the shortest time humanly possible.

When you activate your free membership below, I'll show you the easiest way in the world to create world-class sales copy –the kind that gets real results like this–quickly, easily, and without paying an expensive copywriter like me hundreds of thousands of dollars...

WritingRiches.com

BUY A SHARE OF THE FUTURE IN YOUR COMMUNITY

These certificates make great holiday, graduation and birthday gifts that can be personalized with the recipient's name. The cost of one S.H.A.R.E. or one square foot is $54.17. The personalized certificate is suitable for framing and will state the number of shares purchased and the amount of each share, as well as the recipient's name. The home that you participate in "building" will last for many years and will continue to grow in value.

Here is a sample SHARE certificate:

YES, I WOULD LIKE TO HELP!

I support the work that Habitat for Humanity does and I want to be part of the excitement! As a donor, I will receive periodic updates on your construction activities but, more importantly, I know my gift will help a family in our community realize the dream of homeownership. **I would like to SHARE in your efforts against substandard housing in my community!** *(Please print below)*

PLEASE SEND ME _____ SHARES at $54.17 EACH = $ $_____

In Honor Of: _____

Occasion: (Circle One)   *HOLIDAY*   *BIRTHDAY*   *ANNIVERSARY*

      OTHER: _____

Address of Recipient: _____

Gift From: _____ *Donor Address:* _____

Donor Email: _____

I AM ENCLOSING A CHECK FOR $ $_____ PAYABLE TO HABITAT FOR HUMANITY <u>OR</u> PLEASE CHARGE MY VISA OR MASTERCARD *(CIRCLE ONE)*

Card Number _____ Expiration Date: _____

Name as it appears on Credit Card _____ Charge Amount $ _____

Signature _____

Billing Address _____

Telephone # Day _____ Eve _____

PLEASE NOTE: Your contribution is tax-deductible to the fullest extent allowed by law.
Habitat for Humanity • P.O. Box 1443 • Newport News, VA 23601 • 757-596-5553
www.HelpHabitatforHumanity.org

LaVergne, TN USA
15 February 2011
216569LV00003B/122/P